IN THE KITCHEN WITH KATE

Heart of the Home Recipes
Volume 3

CAPPER PRESS
Topeka, Kansas

Edited by Samantha Adams
Recipes Compiled and Edited
by Rosemary Rebek and Cathy Kofoid
Editorial Assistant: Patricia Thompson
Illustrations by Bruce Bealmear

ISBN 0-941678-49-0

Printed in the United States of America

Foreword

If only I had cut that recipe out of *Capper's* ...

If you're a *Capper's* reader, chances are you've uttered those words at one time or another. After all, *Capper's* cooks are the best anywhere, and in issue after issue they proudly share their best recipes with fellow readers. If you've tried a "Heart of the Home" recipe before, whether it was a delectable pie or a delicious main dish, chances are your family raved about your cooking. And you would make that dish again, if only you had the recipe.

For every reader who has faced this dilemma, *Capper's* is proud to introduce *In the Kitchen with Kate*, the third collection of recipes from the "Heart of the Home." Every year we receive hundreds of top-notch recipes, many of which are requested again. It was hard to choose, but we listened to readers' requests and came up with several categories that best represent the foods our readers love to prepare and eat. The mouth-watering results are evident in the pages that follow.

In addition to recipes, this cookbook includes some extras that every cook can use. You'll find charts that will help you better understand food labels and assist you in converting one type of measurement to another, such as teaspoons to cups or pints to ounces. And because cooking shouldn't be all work, we've also included some of the best food-related poems from the pages of "Heart of the Home." These light-hearted verses are sure to rekindle your best culinary memories.

We hope you enjoy fixing these recipes as much as we did compiling them. Tell your family to prepare their taste buds for something delicious, and don't be surprised when they ask for seconds.

Samantha Adams
Editor

In the Kitchen with Kate
Heart of the Home Recipes Volume 3

Contents

BOUNTIFUL BREADS 7

CONFECTIONARY
DELIGHTS 25

COOKIES
GALORE 35

SAVORY
MAIN DISHES 57

ON THE SIDE 85

MOUTH-WATERING
CAKES 105

DESSERTS
THAT PLEASE 137

PIES FOR
ALL SEASONS 155

APPETIZERS AND EXTRAS 173

Nutrient Content
Labeling Claims Definitions . . .186

Table of Equivalents 187

INDEX 193

Bountiful Breads

■ Bountiful Breads ■

English Muffin Loaves 9
Irish Freckle Bread 9
Banana Macadamia Nut Bread 10
Cranberry-Walnut Loaf 11
Zucchini Bread 11
Raspberry Cereal Bread 12
Apple Butter Bread 12
Pork and Bean Bread 13
Quick Apple Bread 13
Pear Bread 14
Pecan Bread 14
Broccoli Corn Bread 15
Low Cholesterol Bran Bread 15
Eggnog Bread 16
Lime Tea Bread 16
Poppy Seed Bread 17
My Custard Corn Bread 17
Pumpkin-Oat Muffins 18
Strawberry-Rhubarb Muffins 18
Dorathea's Oat Muffins 19
Squash Muffins 19
Lemon Poppy Seed Muffins 20
Ice Cream Muffins 20
Morning Glory Muffins 21
Old-Fashioned Praline Pecan Rolls 21
Overnight Coffeecake 22
Oven Baked Doughnuts 22
Apple Doughnuts 23
Sweet Potato Biscuits 23
Country Ham Biscuits 24
Momovers 24

English Muffin Loaves

This is delicious toasted and served with honey.

2 pkgs. active dry yeast
6 cups unsifted flour
2 tsps. salt
¼ tsp. baking soda
1 Tbsp. honey
2 cups milk
½ cup water
• corn meal

Combine yeast, 3 cups flour, salt and soda. Heat honey, milk and water until very warm. Add to yeast mixture; beat well. Stir in rest of flour to make a stiff batter. Spoon into two 8½x4½-inch greased pans. Sprinkle top with corn meal. Cover; let rise in warm place for 45 minutes. Bake in 400° oven for 25 minutes. Remove from pans immediately and cool. Makes 2 loaves.

Charlene Franta
Donnellson, Iowa
September 30, 1986

Irish Freckle Bread

How about serving the family and friends an old-time Irish bread?

4 cups all-purpose flour
¼ cup granulated sugar
1 tsp. salt
1 tsp. baking powder
¼ cup margarine
2 cups currants OR raisins
1½ cups buttermilk
1 egg
1 tsp. soda

Sift flour, granulated sugar, salt and baking powder. Cut in margarine to resemble coarse corn meal. Stir in currants or raisins. Combine buttermilk, beaten egg and soda. Stir liquid mixture into dry mixture until just moist. Put in greased loaf pan; cut gash across the top in form of a cross. Bake in 375° oven 45-50 minutes, or until golden brown. Cool on rack before cutting.

Clara Young
Oxford, Kansas
March 13, 1990

HOW LONG SHOULD YOU KNEAD BREAD?
To determine if bread dough has been kneaded enough, push a finger into the dough. The dough should "spring" back to its original shape.

Banana Macadamia Nut Bread

2 cups all-purpose flour
¾ cup granulated sugar
½ cup butter, softened
2 eggs
1 tsp. baking soda
½ tsp. salt
1 Tbsp. grated orange peel
1 tsp. vanilla
1 cup (2 medium) mashed ripe bananas
¼ cup orange juice
1 cup flaked coconut
¾ cup (3½-oz. jar) coarsely chopped macadamia nuts OR walnuts

In large bowl combine flour, granulated sugar, butter, eggs, baking soda, salt, grated orange peel and vanilla. Beat at low speed, scraping bowl often, until well mixed (2 or 3 minutes).

Add bananas and orange juice. Continue beating and scraping the bowl often, until well mixed, about 1 minute.

By hand, stir in coconut and nuts. Batter will be thick. Spread into 3 greased 3x5½-inch mini-loaf pans or 1 greased 9x5-inch loaf pan.

Bake in preheated 350° oven. Bake mini-loaves 35-45 minutes; large loaf 60-65 minutes or until wooden pick inserted in center comes out clean. Cool 10 minutes; remove from pan(s).

Kate Marchbanks Food Story
December 7, 1993

■ Kneading Dough ■

Flour sprinkled on a table top
And a wash pan full of dough.
She hummed her favorite hymn,
Pinched the sticky ball,
Then gingerly turned it out.
Heel to toe, to and fro
She rocked in steady rhythm,
Humming, kneading, folding.
Nimble fingers, practiced fingers
Expertly shaping the dough
As she had for many, many years;
But still modestly insisting her
Secret ingredient for good bread
Is a good hymn.

— **Pamela Forsberg**

Cranberry-Walnut Loaf

This makes delicious bread.

2 cups all-purpose flour
¾ cup granulated sugar
1½ tsps. baking powder
½ tsp. baking soda
½ tsp. salt
1 large egg
1 Tbsp. grated orange rind
⅓ cup orange juice
¼ cup (½ stick) butter
¼ cup milk
1½ cups fresh cranberries, halved
½ cup chopped walnuts

In large bowl, combine flour, granulated sugar, baking powder, baking soda and salt. In small bowl, combine egg, orange rind and juice. In small saucepan, melt butter. Remove from heat; stir in milk. Set aside.

Grease and flour a 9x5-inch loaf pan. Preheat oven to 350°. Stir egg mixture and butter mixture into dry ingredients just until flour is moistened. Fold in cranberries and nuts.

Spread batter in prepared pan. Bake 50 minutes, or until cake tester inserted in center comes out clean. Cool in pan on wire rack 10 minutes. Remove from pan; cool loaf completely. Wrap and store overnight before slicing. Makes 1 loaf.

Joan Dixon
Westmont, Illinois
March 2, 1993

Zucchini Bread

This is a favorite of my entire family. I made more than 50 loaves last winter!

3 large eggs
2 cups granulated sugar
2 tsps. vanilla (optional)
1 cup vegetable oil
2 cups grated zucchini
1 cup crushed pineapple, drained
3 cups flour
1 tsp. baking soda
1 tsp. baking powder
1 tsp. cinnamon
½ tsp. allspice
3 cups nuts, raisins, chopped dates and candied fruit

Beat eggs until fluffy. Add granulated sugar, a little at a time. Add vanilla, oil, zucchini and pineapple a little at a time. Mix together flour, baking soda, baking powder, cinnamon and allspice and add to zucchini mixture a little at a time. Stir in mixture of fruit and nuts. Pour into 2 greased, floured loaf pans. Bake in 350° oven for 1 hour or until done. Test with a toothpick and bake longer if necessary. Let set on rack for 10 minutes before removing from pans. Cool thoroughly.

Loaves can be wrapped and frozen for weeks.

Mrs. Olivia M. Wiese
Davenport, Iowa
October 25, 1994

Raspberry Cereal Bread

This is delicious as a bread or may be baked in muffin pans!

1 cup fresh rasp-
  berries
¾ cup Grapenuts
1¼ cups milk
½ cup granulated
  sugar
1 egg
2 cups flour
2 tsps. baking powder
½ tsp. salt

Sort and wash berries. Soak Grapenuts in milk for 15 minutes; add granulated sugar and well-beaten egg. Mix and sift dry ingredients and add to final mixture. Mix just enough to blend thoroughly. Carefully fold in raspberries. Pour into a large greased loaf pan. Bake in 350° oven for 1 hour. To make muffins, use 1¾ cups flour and bake in a moderate oven for 35 minutes.

Mrs. Opal Couch
Nebraska
July 2, 1947

Apple Butter Bread

2 cups flour
1 tsp. baking powder
1 tsp. baking soda
½ tsp. nutmeg
1 tsp. salt
1 cup chopped nuts
1 beaten egg
¾ cup granulated
  sugar
1 cup apple butter
¼ cup oil

Sift flour, baking powder, baking soda, nutmeg and salt into a large bowl. Stir in nuts. Combine egg, granulated sugar, apple butter and oil and add to dry ingredients, stirring until blended. Pour into a 9x5-inch greased loaf pan. Bake in 350° oven for about 50 minutes, or until done.

Mildred Sherrer
Bay City, Texas
October 8, 1991

■ Nature's Shop ■

It's easy to tell when autumn's at hand
For everyone opens a roadside fruit stand.
Bright orange pumpkins in mountainous stacks.
All kinds of apples in brown paper sacks,
Wreaths of grapevines and dried flowers galore,
Make every crossroads a marvelous store.
There's amber wheat braids with calico bows,
And crooked necked gourds in uneven rows.
Who can resist the temptation to stop
When nature supplies such a beautiful shop.

— Bess Michael

Pork and Bean Bread

The raisins in this recipe should be drained and added as the last ingredient.

1 cup raisins
1 cup boiling water
3 eggs
1 cup oil
2 cups granulated sugar
1 16-oz. can pork and beans
3 cups flour
1 tsp. cinnamon
½ tsp. baking powder
1 tsp. baking soda
½ tsp. salt
1 tsp. vanilla
1 cup nuts

Mix raisins with boiling water. Stir and set aside. Beat eggs, oil, granulated sugar and pork and beans until beans are broken. Add flour and remaining dry ingredients to bean mixture. Add nuts and vanilla. Drain raisins and add, stirring to mix well. Pour batter into 3 well-greased loaf pans. Bake in 325° oven for 50-60 minutes.

Mildred Sherrer
Bay City, Texas
July 19, 1983

Quick Apple Bread

This bread makes tasty little sandwiches to serve with fruit salad.

½ cup shortening
1 cup granulated sugar
2 eggs
1 cup ground, OR finely chopped, unpeeled apples
1½ Tbsps. of butter-milk OR sour cream
1 tsp. vanilla
½ tsp. salt
1 tsp. baking soda
1 tsp. baking powder
2 cups flour
1 cup chopped walnuts OR pecans

Cream shortening and granulated sugar, then beat in eggs. Add apples, buttermilk and vanilla. Sift dry ingredients together several times and add to first mixture. Add nuts. Bake in well-greased bread loaf pan. Bake in 350° oven 50-60 minutes or until cake tester comes out clean.

Mrs. Helen Rebic
McAllen, Texas
November 10, 1992

Pear Bread

This is a real good treat, so moist and tasty. Everyone likes it.

½ cup butter
1 cup granulated sugar
2 eggs
2 cups flour
½ tsp. salt
½ tsp. baking soda
1 tsp. baking powder
⅛ tsp. nutmeg
¼ cup yogurt OR buttermilk
1 cup coarsely chopped, peeled pears
1 tsp. vanilla

Cream butter, granulated sugar and eggs. Combine dry ingredients and add to egg mixture with buttermilk. Stir in pears and vanilla. Pour into buttered 5x9x3-inch pan. Bake in 350° oven for 1 hour.

Mrs. Gladys Beer
Topeka, Kansas
September 19, 1985

Pecan Bread

This is a favorite of ours.

¼ cup margarine
½ cup brown sugar
1 egg
2 tsps. grated orange peel
2 cups flour
2 tsps. baking powder
½ tsp. salt
¾ cup orange juice
½ cup chopped pecans

Cream margarine and brown sugar with an electric mixer until light and fluffy. Beat in egg and orange peel. Combine flour, baking powder and salt. At low speed, alternately beat in flour mixture and orange juice. Stir in pecans. Turn batter into a greased 8½x4½-inch loaf pan. Bake at 350° for 50 minutes or until pick inserted in middle comes out clean.

Mrs. Anna J. Nicholls
Decatur, Illinois
December 5, 1989

PUMPKIN TRICKS

Many cookbook authors use pumpkin in their recipes to add moisture, acidity, texture, color and flavor.

To enhance the flavor of pumpkin, some chefs use maple syrup, crystallized ginger, molasses, freshly ground pepper, coriander or cardamom.

Pumpkin soup is a traditional favorite in the fall harvest season in many parts of the country. It can actually be served in a small, hollowed-out pumpkin.

Broccoli Corn Bread

My family and friends just love this corn bread. It is so simple to make and makes plenty.

½ cup margarine, melted
⅓ cup chopped onion
1 tsp. salt
¾ cup cottage cheese
1 10-oz. pkg. frozen broccoli, chopped
4 eggs, slightly beaten
1 8½-oz. pkg. corn muffin mix

Thaw and drain broccoli. In mixing bowl, combine everything but corn muffin mix. Stir muffin mix into first mixture. Pour into a greased 9x13x2-inch pan. Bake in 400° oven for 20 minutes.

Mary Newell
Oskaloosa, Kansas
September 1, 1992

Low Cholesterol Bran Bread

If you are watching your cholesterol as well as sugar, this is the bread for you.

1 cup bran cereal
⅔ cup oil
1 Tbsp. diet sugar
2 tsps. salt
1 cup hot water
2 pkgs. yeast
1 cup lukewarm water
6½ cups flour
2 egg whites, well beaten

Place bran, oil, diet sugar and salt in hot water. Dissolve yeast in lukewarm water and add to bran mixture. Add 3 cups flour. Beat well. Fold in beaten egg whites and add remaining flour. Knead until smooth. Place in greased bowl, turn dough and grease top. Cover with towel and let stand in warm place until double.

Punch down and let rise again, about 15-20 minutes. Turn out onto floured surface and knead about 5 minutes. Divide dough and place in well-greased pans. Cover and let rise until double. Bake in preheated 400° oven for 15 minutes. Reduce heat to 350° and bake until well browned, 35-45 minutes **TOTAL** baking time. For a tender crust, brush loaves with margarine 3 or 4 minutes before removing from oven.

Mrs. Eilene Metcalf
Bauxite, Arkansas
April 25, 1989

Eggnog Bread

This is just perfect for the holidays.

3   cups all-purpose flour
½   cup granulated sugar
4   tsps. baking powder
½   tsp. salt
½   tsp. ground nutmeg
1   beaten egg
1¾ cups canned OR dairy eggnog
½   cup cooking oil
½   cup chopped pecans
½   cup golden raisins
½   cup sifted powdered sugar
2-3 tsps. eggnog

In a large mixing bowl, stir together flour, granulated sugar, baking powder, salt and nutmeg. Combine egg, eggnog and oil; add to dry ingredients, stirring just until combined. Stir in nuts and raisins and turn into greased 9x5x3-inch loaf pan. Bake in 350° oven for 60-70 minutes. Cover with foil after 50 minutes if bread browns too quickly. Cool in pan for 10 minutes. Remove bread from pan; cool on rack.

Wrap bread; store overnight. To serve, stir together powdered sugar and enough eggnog to make mixture of drizzling consistency. Drizzle over bread. Makes 1 loaf or 16 servings.

Louise W. Mayer
Richmond, Virginia
December 8, 1992

Lime Tea Bread

This bread is delicious in the summer. Serve with a tall glass of lemonade or limeade. Hope you all enjoy this.

6   Tbsps. softened butter
¾   cup granulated sugar
2   large eggs
2   cups all-purpose flour
2   tsps. baking powder
½   tsp. salt
⅔   cup milk
1   tsp. grated lime peel
2   Tbsps. lime juice
2   Tbsps. finely chopped, fresh mint
•   powdered sugar

Grease and flour 8½x4½-inch loaf pan. In large bowl, beat butter and granulated sugar with electric mixer until fluffy. Beat in eggs until well mixed. In bowl, combine flour, baking powder and salt. Add flour and milk alternately into butter mixture at a low speed until blended. Beat in lime peel, lime juice and mint. Pour into loaf pan and bake in preheated 325° oven for 50 minutes or until skewer inserted in center comes out clean. Cool in pan on rack for 10 minutes. Remove from pan. Cool on rack and wrap. Before serving, dust bread with powdered sugar and slice. Makes 1 loaf.

Mrs. Peggy Hughley
New York, New York
July 31, 1990

Poppy Seed Bread

This is a good holiday bread.

3 eggs, beaten
1⅛ cups cooking oil
2¼ cups granulated
    sugar
3 cups flour
1 tsp. salt
1½ tsps. baking powder
2 Tbsps. poppy seed
1½ cups milk
1½ tsps. butter
1½ tsps. almond extract
1½ tsps. vanilla extract

Topping:
¾ cup granulated
   sugar
¼ cup concentrated
   orange juice
   (undiluted)
½ tsp. butter flavoring
½ tsp. vanilla flavoring

Beat eggs. Add oil and beat with hand egg beater. Add other ingredients and mix by hand. Pour into 2 large, greased loaf pans or 3 medium greased loaf pans. Bake in 350° oven for 1 hour. While loaves are hot, poke holes with a toothpick and pour topping over them.

To make topping, mix granulated sugar, orange juice and flavorings. Pour over bread.

Juaneta Heckman
Ottawa, Kansas
December 19, 1989

My Custard Corn Bread

I have made this recipe since 1945 and believe that this is better than the one Capper's *published in the September 29, 1987, issue.*

2 eggs
½ cup granulated
   sugar
1 cup milk
1 cup sour milk OR
   buttermilk
1 tsp. baking soda
1½ cups corn meal
½ cup flour
1 tsp. salt
2 Tbsps. butter
1 cup milk

Beat eggs. Add granulated sugar and mix thoroughly. Add the first cup of sweet milk. Dissolve soda in sour milk and add to egg mixture. Mix corn meal with flour and salt and add to mixture, beating until smooth. Melt 2 tablespoons butter in shallow 8x13-inch pan and pour in batter. Pour 1 cup milk over top, but do not stir. Place at once in 400° oven and bake for about 30 minutes. A delicious custard will form over the top of the soft corn bread. Serve hot with butter.

Blanche Erbert
Ellis, Kansas
October 10, 1989

Pumpkin-Oat Muffins

If you are trying to lower cho-lesterol, these are good, espe-cially served warm for breakfast.

- 1⅓ cups oat bran
- 1 cup rolled oats
- 1¼ cups skimmed milk
- ¾ cup whole-wheat flour
- ½ cup brown sugar
- 1 Tbsp. baking powder
- ½ tsp. nutmeg
- ½ tsp. ginger
- 2 tsps. cinnamon
- ¾ cup canned OR cooked pumpkin (cooked butternut squash may be used instead)
- 2 egg whites OR ¼ cup egg substitute
- 2 Tbsps. vegetable oil
- ½ cup raisins

Combine bran, rolled oats and milk in a bowl. In another bowl, mix flour, brown sugar, baking powder and spices (3 teaspoons pumpkin pie spice may be substituted). Blend pumpkin, egg whites, oil and raisins in a third bowl, then add to oat-milk mixture. Add the flour-sugar mixture and stir contents just until moist.

Grease 12 or more muffin tins with vegetable oil spray and divide the batter equally among them. Bake in preheat-ed 400° oven for 20-25 min-utes, or until lightly browned.

Lela Eberle
York, Nebraska
January 3, 1989

Strawberry-Rhubarb Muffins

This is one of my favorites in the spring.

- 1¾ cup flour
- ½ cup granulated sugar
- 2½ tsps. baking powder
- ½ tsp. salt
- 1 egg, beaten
- ¾ cup milk
- ½ cup vegetable oil
- ¾ cup minced rhubarb
- ½ cup sliced strawberries
- 6 strawberries, cut in half

Mix flour, granulated sugar, baking powder and salt. Combine egg, milk and oil in a small bowl and stir into flour mixture with a fork until just moistened. Fold in rhubarb and sliced berries. Fill well-buttered or lined muffin cups ⅔ full. Gently press a berry half into the top of each muffin. Sprinkle tops generously with granulat-ed sugar. Bake until golden brown in 400° oven for 20-25 minutes. Remove from pan and cool on racks. Makes 12 muffins.

Mrs. P.B. Brothers
Richmond, Virginia
May 23, 1989

Dorathea's Oat Muffins

I always have these muffins on hand. As soon as they are all eaten I make another batch.

1 cup raisins
1 cup skim milk
1 Tbsp. vinegar
2 cups oat bran
1 cup 100% bran cereal
1 Tbsp. baking powder
¼ cup honey OR sugar substitute to taste
1 Tbsp. unsaturated oil
½ container egg substitute OR 1 egg

Add vinegar to skim milk. Cover raisins with water and add the skim milk. Let stand 5 minutes. Mix together oat bran, 100% bran and baking powder. Add honey or sugar substitute, oil and egg or substitute. Stir in raisin-milk mixture.

Spray or grease cupcake pans and pour in batter, filling ¾ full. Bake 15-17 minutes in preheated 375-400° oven. Remove from oven to rack and let stand 1-2 minutes. Remove from pans onto cooling rack. Store in freezer bag in refrigerator. They will keep at least a week.

Dorathea J. Bath
Sussex, New Jersey
January 30, 1990

Squash Muffins

Yellow squash stars in these muffins.

2 cups all-purpose flour
1 Tbsp. baking powder
¼ tsp. salt
2 Tbsps. granulated sugar
⅔ cup yellow squash, grated
1 egg, beaten
¾ cup milk
2 Tbsps. vegetable oil

Combine flour, baking powder, salt, granulated sugar and squash in large bowl; make a well in center of mixture. Combine egg, milk and oil; add to dry ingredients, stirring just until moistened. Spoon batter into lightly greased muffin pans, filling ⅔ full.

Bake at 350° for 20-25 minutes. Remove from pans immediately. Makes 1 dozen muffins.

Monnie Sullivan
Lillington, North Carolina
August 16, 1994

Lemon Poppy Seed Muffins

These are wonderful muffins!

1   pkg. lemon cake mix
1   pkg. instant lemon pudding mix
1   cup water
½   cup oil
4   eggs
¼   cup poppy seeds

Heat oven to 350°. Mix all ingredients together thoroughly. Line muffin tins with paper liners and fill ½-⅔ full. Bake for 25 minutes.

M.L. Willard
Mission, Kansas
February 15, 1994

Ice Cream Muffins

Here is something different to try.

1   cup self-rising flour
1   cup vanilla ice cream

Preheat oven to 350°. Mix flour and ice cream together and turn into greased muffin tins. Bake 12 minutes.

Monica Turk
Milwaukee, Wisconsin
April 25, 1989

■ Bread and Patches ■

My mother baked the bread each day
That kept her family fed,
And every time she set the yeast
A thousand prayers were said.

And even though she'd rather read
—Each day she'd mend our clothes,
And while she sewed the patches on
A million prayers arose.

My mother's bread was always good.
She leavened it with truth.
And her patches always kept us warm
—They healed the hearts of youth.

The bread that she baked is still
Feeding my soul,
And her patches of prayer are still
Keeping me whole.

— Tilitha Waicekauskas

Morning Glory Muffins

This muffin recipe tastes good and is healthy, too. The muffins also freeze well.

2 cups whole wheat flour
1½ cups white flour
1 cup brown sugar
4 tsps. soda
1 tsp. salt
2 tsps. cinnamon
1 tsp. nutmeg
1 cup honey
⅔ cup vegetable oil
1 cup milk
4 eggs, beaten
2 tsps. vanilla
¾ cup raisins
3 cups shredded carrots
1½ cups chopped nuts OR coconut

In large bowl stir together wheat flour and white flour, brown sugar, soda, salt, cinnamon and nutmeg. In another bowl, stir together honey, oil, milk, beaten egg and vanilla. Make a well in center of dry ingredients. Add honey mixture and stir just to combine. Stir in raisins, carrots, nuts or coconut. Line muffin cups with cupcake papers. Spoon batter into muffin cups, filling almost full. Bake at 350° for 15-20 minutes until toothpick comes out clean. Makes about 2 dozen muffins.

Joan Englin
Alexandria, Minnesota
July 19, 1994

Old-Fashioned Praline Pecan Rolls

1 lb. loaf of frozen bread dough
½ cup butter OR margarine, melted
¼ cup brown sugar
½ cup pecan halves

Filling:
⅔ cup chopped pecans
½ cup brown sugar
2 Tbsps. flour

Bread dough may be thawed in the refrigerator overnight or in the microwave on LOW for 6 minutes. Place 4 tablespoons melted butter in bottom of a well-greased 9x13-inch cake pan. Sprinkle ¼ cup brown sugar and ½ cup pecan halves over butter. On a lightly floured board, roll dough out to a 10x14-inch rectangle. Brush with 2 tablespoons melted butter. Combine filling ingredients and sprinkle evenly over dough. Beginning with 10-inch side, roll dough up tightly in jelly-roll fashion. Pinch dough along edge to seal. Slice rolled dough into 12 pieces. Place slices cut-side down in prepared pan. Brush dough with remaining butter. Let rise until rolls have doubled in size (2-3 hours). Bake in a 350° oven for 25 minutes or until golden brown. Carefully invert rolls onto serving platter at once (syrup is very hot). Makes 12 rolls.

Kate Marchbanks Food Story
January 31, 1989

Overnight Coffeecake

This is delicious and convenient. My guests always want the recipe.

2 cups flour
1 tsp. baking powder
1 tsp. baking soda
1 tsp. cinnamon
½ tsp. salt
⅔ cup margarine
1 cup granulated sugar
½ cup brown sugar
2 eggs
1 cup buttermilk

Topping:
½ cup brown sugar
½ cup chopped nuts
1 tsp. cinnamon
1 tsp. nutmeg

Sift flour, baking powder, baking soda, cinnamon and salt together and set aside. Cream margarine, granulated sugar and brown sugar. Add eggs and beat well. Add dry ingredients alternately with buttermilk and spread in well-greased 9x13-inch pan.
Mix topping ingredients together and spread on top of batter. Cover pan with foil and refrigerate 8 hours. Bake in preheated 350° oven for approximately 45 minutes.

Mrs. Bennie Peters
Greensburg, Kansas
May 24, 1988

Oven Baked Doughnuts

These are simple and perhaps healthier, as they are not fried.

Doughnuts:
½ cup granulated sugar
2½ Tbsps. shortening
2 eggs
2 cups flour
2 tsps. nutmeg
½ tsp. salt
2 tsps. baking powder
6 Tbsps. milk

Coating:
½ cup melted butter
½ cup granulated sugar
1 tsp. cinnamon, OR to taste

For doughnuts: blend granulated sugar and shortening together well. Add eggs, flour, nutmeg, salt, baking powder and milk, stirring well. Using an ice cream scoop, put in greased muffin tins. Bake at 400° for 15-20 minutes. Remove from oven and from pans and dip into ½ cup melted butter, then into granulated sugar and cinnamon mixture. Makes about 12.

Mrs. Ruth Drexler
Fairbury, Nebraska
February 1, 1994

Apple Doughnuts

This is a favorite of my family and the first recipe I want to make when the weather cools.

- 3 cups flour
- ⅛ tsp. salt
- 1 tsp. nutmeg
- 4 tsps. baking powder
- 1 cup granulated sugar
- ⅔ cup shortening
- 2 eggs, beaten
- ½ cup milk
- 1 cup peeled and grated apples

Mix the flour, salt, nutmeg, baking powder and granulated sugar together. Cut in shortening. Add combined eggs, milk and apples, mixing just enough to moisten. Spoon into greased muffin tins, filling ½ full. Bake in 350° oven 20-25 minutes.

Remove from pan and while hot, dip into melted margarine or butter (1 stick), then into a mixture of ½ cup granulated sugar and 1 tablespoon cinnamon.

Mary Newell
Oskaloosa, Kansas
November 7, 1989

Sweet Potato Biscuits

I'm 83 years old and love to try new recipes, but some of my old ones are real good.

- 1 cup flour
- 3 tsps. baking powder
- ½ tsp. salt
- 4 Tbsps. shortening
- 1 cup cooked, mashed sweet potatoes
- ½-¾ cup milk

Sift flour, baking powder and salt together. Add shortening and sweet potatoes. Stir in enough milk to make a stiff dough. Roll out dough and cut. Bake in hot 400° oven for 20-30 minutes.

Carrie Treichel
Johnson City, Tennessee
October 9, 1990

■ Toast to Toast ■

*Of course
that's why we toast bread...
For the aroma
Yeasty fumes fill my nostrils*

*I see
fields of wheat, oats, and rye
waving in the wind*

*Fifty pound flowered sacks
of flour*

*Loaves of fresh-baked bread
on kitchen table*

Daily bread.

— Lee Brezina

Country Ham Biscuits

These are a treat anytime!

2 cups flour
1 Tbsp. baking powder
½ cup minced, cooked
country ham
3 Tbsps. shortening
¾ cup milk

Sift together flour and baking powder in large bowl. Stir in ham. Cut in shortening with knife until mixture resembles coarse crumbs. Add milk. Gather into ball with fork. Pat dough to ¼-inch thickness on floured board. Cut out with floured biscuit cutter, about 2½ inches in diameter. Put on ungreased baking sheet. Bake in 450° oven until golden, about 12-15 minutes.

Sandy Simianer
Scottsbluff, Nebraska
January 21, 1992

Momovers

Such as Pop never made.

⅔ cup flour
¼ tsp. salt
⅓ cup milk
⅓ cup water
2 eggs
½ cup shredded
sharp Cheddar
cheese
4 Tbsps. butter OR
margarine

Preheat oven to 375°. In medium bowl, mix flour and salt. Add milk and water and mix well. Beat in eggs. Fold cheese in last. Place 1 tablespoon butter or margarine in each of four 8-ounce oven-proof custard cups. Put cups on cookie sheet and place in oven for 4-5 minutes, or until butter or margarine melts. Remove from oven. With a pastry brush, coat inside of cup well.

Fill cups ½ full with batter and bake 45-50 minutes. Avoid peeking until toward the end. Make sure they are nice and brown so they won't deflate.

Serve with sweet butter. Makes 4. Easily doubled.

Mrs. L.W. Mayer
Richmond, Virginia
January 4, 1994

Confectionary Delights

■ Confectionary Delights ■

Fudgy Bonbons 27
Flake Candy 28
Colonial Peanut Butter Fudge 28
Sorghum Divinity 29
Cheese Spread Fudge 29
Honey Candy 30
Bun Candy 30
Matilda's Divinity 31
Apricot Nuggets 31
Orange-Butterscotch Walnut Clusters .32
Two-Flavor Fudge 32
White Fruited Fudge 33

Fudgy Bonbons

A Pillsbury BAKE-OFF winner.

- 2 cups semi-sweet chocolate chips
- ¼ cup butter OR margarine
- 1 14-oz. can sweet-ened condensed milk (not evaporated)
- 2 cups all-purpose OR unbleached flour*
- ½ cup finely chopped nuts, if desired
- 1 tsp. vanilla
- 60 milk chocolate candy kisses OR white and choco-late-striped candy kisses, unwrapped
- 1 2-oz. white baking bar OR vanilla-fla-vored candy coating
- 1 tsp. shortening OR oil

Heat oven to 350°. In medium saucepan, combine chocolate chips and butter; cook and stir over very low heat until chips are melted and smooth. Add sweetened condensed milk; mix well. Lightly spoon flour into measuring cup; level off. In medium bowl, combine flour, nuts, chocolate mixture and vanilla; mix well. Shape 1 tablespoonful (use measuring spoon) of dough around each candy kiss, covering complete-ly. Place 1 inch apart on ungreased cookie sheets.

Bake for 6-8 minutes. Cookies will be soft and appear shiny, but become firm as they cool. Do not overbake. Remove from cookie sheets; cool.

In small saucepan, combine white baking bar and shorten-ing; cook and stir over low heat until melted and smooth. Drizzle over cookies. Store in tightly covered container. Makes 5 dozen cookies.

*In high altitudes, above 3,500 feet, increase flour to 2¼ cups and bake as directed.

Kate Marchbanks Food Story March 15, 1994

DUSTY CHOCOLATE
Chocolate can form a white or grayish dusty film called "bloom" when stored at a warm temperature. Bloom does not affect quality or flavor of chocolate and will "disappear" when chocolate is melted or used in baking.

■ WHEN MAILING CANDIES ...
Do not package candies that absorb moisture in the same container as those that lose moisture. Use a heavy cardboard box or coffee can as a mailing container with crumbled or shredded newspaper or plastic filler for padding. Mark the package "FRAGILE" to ensure careful handling.

Flake Candy

This is one of my favorites!

1 cup white syrup
1 cup granulated sugar
1 cup cream
5 cups cornflakes
3 cups crispy rice cereal
2 cups salted, roasted peanuts
1 cup coconut

Combine syrup, granulated sugar and cream in a saucepan and cook to soft ball stage. Mix with the cornflakes, rice cereal, peanuts and coconut. Put in buttered pan, cool and cut.

Mary Beth Yutzy
Fairbank, Iowa
January 17, 1989

Colonial Peanut Butter Fudge

This is so easy and so good!

4 cups powdered sugar
¼ tsp. salt
1 cup peanut butter
½ cup white corn syrup
1 stick (4 ozs.) margarine, melted
1 Tbsp. vanilla
1 cup nuts (optional)

Mix ingredients and press into buttered pan. Refrigerate.

Elmer Tuttle Church
Yukon, West Virginia
November 6, 1990

■ Summertime ■

Comes Maytime and June time,
and then comes summer's heat,
with sunning time,
and swimming time,
and ice-cream cones to eat.
Comes ice time,
and lemonade time,
and time that is so sweet,
time for music in the park
and neighbors there to meet.
Hot dog and corn cob time,
watermelon cut with a knife,
and sleeping out-of-doors time,
the best time of my life.

— Joy Hewitt Mann

Sorghum Divinity

This divinity is delicious and different for your Christmas boxes.

Use 1 cup sorghum, 3 cups granulated sugar, 1½ cups sweet cream, ¼ cup nuts and 1 teaspoon vanilla.

Put sorghum, granulated sugar and cream in saucepan and boil until almost hard ball stage, stirring all the time.

Remove from the stove, add vanilla and nutmeats. Beat until very creamy, then pour out in well-greased pans. Cool (refrigerate), and just before the candy is cold, dip a knife in cold water and mark squares.

Mrs. J.P.
Oklahoma
December 9, 1939

Cheese Spread Fudge

This is delicious, as well as easy to make.

½ lb. pasteurized cheese spread, cubed
1 cup margarine
2 lbs. powdered sugar
½ cup cocoa
3 cups chopped pecans
1 tsp. vanilla

Heat cheese and margarine in 3-quart saucepan over low heat, stirring occasionally until melted. Gradually add combined sifted sugar and cocoa, stirring until smooth. Add pecans and vanilla; mix well. Spread into greased 9x13-inch pan. Cover and chill. Cut into squares.

Clara Young
Oxford, Kansas
December 21, 1993

CAREFUL STORING MAKES DELICIOUS CANDIES
Individually wrap candies in waxed paper or plastic wrap; nearly all candies will stay fresher longer.

Store individually wrapped candies in boxes, tins or cartons with tight-fitting lids. The exception is small hard candies, which should be stored together in a tightly fitting jar after dusting with finely ground (not powdered) sugar.

Do not mix candies that absorb moisture, such as caramels, mints and hard candies, in the same container as those that lose moisture—fudge, fondants, meringues. Use waxed paper to individually wrap or separate layers of fudge to avoid sticking.

Honey Candy

I have a delicious candy recipe that I want to share.

1 cup honey
¾ cup powdered milk
1 cup rolled oats
½ cup peanut butter
½ cup chopped pea-
  nuts OR other nuts
½ cup chocolate chips,
  raisins OR dried
  fruit (optional)

Boil honey for 4 minutes, stirring to keep from burning. Add powdered milk, oats, peanut butter, peanuts and the chips, raisins or dried fruit if desired. Pour into buttered pan. Cut into squares when cool. Wrap in waxed paper.

Bessie Bachman
Federal Way, Washington
December 9, 1986

Bun Candy

These taste remarkably like those delicious round candy bars.

1 12-oz. pkg. choco-
  late chips
1 12-oz. pkg.
  butterscotch chips
1 18-oz. jar creamy
  peanut butter
1 cup butter OR
  margarine
⅔ cup milk
1 3½-oz. pkg. vanilla
  pudding mix (not
  instant)
2 lbs. powdered
  sugar
1 lb. dry roasted
  peanuts

Melt both kinds of chips and the peanut butter in a double boiler. Spread half of mixture in a buttered 10x15-inch pan. Chill.
Cook butter, milk and pudding mix for 1 minute. Add powdered sugar and stir well. Spread over mixture in pan. Chill. Add peanuts to remaining chocolatey mixture and spread over chilled mixture. Refrigerate. Cut into squares. Makes at least 5 pounds of candy.

Mrs. Paul Voigts
Crete, Illinois
March 28, 1989

Matilda's Divinity

This is very good and easy!

- 2 cups granulated sugar
- ½ cup water
- • pinch of salt
- 1 13-oz jar marshmallow creme
- 1 tsp. vanilla
- ½ cup nuts

Boil granulated sugar, water and salt to 250° on a candy thermometer. Put marshmallow creme in a large bowl. Pour sugar-syrup mixture slowly over creme while stirring. Add vanilla and nuts. Pour into an 8x8-inch pan. Cool and cut into pieces.

Matilda Praska
Cresco, Iowa
February 3, 1987

Apricot Nuggets

These easy-to-make candies add a tasty note to a plate of Christmas confections.

- 1 lb. powdered sugar
- 6 Tbsps. melted butter OR margarine
- 2 Tbsps. orange juice
- ½ tsp. vanilla
- 1 11-oz. pkg. dried apricots, ground (about 1½ cups)
- 1 cup chopped pecans

Combine sugar, butter, orange juice and vanilla. Add apricots. Mix, then knead in bowl until ingredients are well mixed. Form into 1-inch balls. Roll in chopped nuts. Store in refrigerator or freezer in covered container. Makes 6 dozen candies.

Elizabeth McJunkin
Toronto, Kansas
December 17, 1991

PLAYING 'DREIDEL'
During the holidays, Jewish families often play "dreidel." Each player has a chance to spin the top-like toy to land on "gimmel," the Hebrew letter meaning "great," and win all of the chocolate coins, gold coins or little treats.

Orange-Butterscotch Walnut Clusters

This is very good candy.

1　3- or 4-oz. pkg. butterscotch pudding and pie filling (not instant)
1　cup granulated sugar
½　cup evaporated milk
½　tsp. grated orange rind
1　Tbsp. butter
1½　cups walnut halves

Blend granulated sugar with pudding mix in a 2-quart saucepan. Stir in evaporated milk and orange rind. Add butter. Cook and stir over medium heat until mixture comes to a boil. Lower heat and boil gently for 3 minutes, stirring constantly. Remove from heat and stir in walnuts. Beat until candy thickens. Drop from teaspoon onto foil or into paper candy cups. Let cool until set. Makes about 32 clusters.

Gladys M. Hanes
Fort Scott, Kansas
October 23, 1990

Two-Flavor Fudge

This is pretty as well as tasty.

2　cups firmly packed brown sugar
1　cup granulated sugar
1　cup evaporated milk
½　cup margarine
1　7-oz. jar marshmallow creme
1　6-oz. pkg. chocolate chips
1　6-oz. pkg. butterscotch chips
2　cups walnuts, divided
2　tsps. vanilla, divided

In saucepan, combine brown sugar, granulated sugar, milk and margarine. Bring to a full boil over moderate heat, stirring frequently. Boil for 15 minutes. Remove from heat. Add marshmallow creme. Divide mixture in half. Add butterscotch chips to one half and chocolate chips to the other. Stir each mixture until chips are melted. Blend 1 teaspoon vanilla and 1 cup walnuts into each half. Pour into greased 9-inch pan, putting 1 half over the other. Chill until firm.

This makes about 2½ pounds.

Sunny Diecker
Duncan, Oklahoma
December 22, 1992

White Fruited Fudge

This recipe came from an old calendar, dating back to the 1960s.

2	**cups granulated sugar**
1	**cup light cream**
¼	**cup butter**
¼	**cup light corn syrup**
½	**tsp. salt**
1	**cup miniature marshmallows**
1	**tsp. vanilla**
½	**cup pecan halves**
⅓	**cup chopped red candied cherries**
⅓	**cup chopped green candied cherries**

Combine granulated sugar, cream, butter, syrup and salt in a large, heavy saucepan, Bring to a gentle boil over low heat. Cook, stirring constantly, until sugar melts. Continue cooking, stirring occasionally until mixture reaches the soft ball stage, 238-240°.

Remove from heat and stir in marshmallows and vanilla. Stir until marshmallows melt and candy starts losing its gloss. Stir in pecan halves and fruit. Stir until candy starts to set. Pour into buttered 8-inch square pan. Cool. Makes 25-30 pieces.

Helen Anastas
Kansas City, Missouri
October 14, 1986

■ 100% Food Free! ■

Today for breakfast I did eat
An artificial egg,
And artificial bacon that
Had never seen a pig,
And imitation coffee,
Containing no caffeine,
With sweetened sugar substitute
And powdered creamless cream,
And toast from bread the label said
Contained no wheat whatever,
But twenty kinds of chemicals
To help it go down better.

My breakfast had no sodium,
Or saturated fat,
Or calories, or nourishment,
Or harmful stuff like that.

Of course you know what's coming,
Next week if not today.
We'll eat the plastic wrappers
And just throw the food away!

— Frank Carson Knebel

■ Diet Guide ■

I like a balanced breakfast
You probably do too
Mine is any number of doughnuts
That's divisible by two!

— Paul G. Swope

■ South Dakota Blizzard ■

Chived potato soup
Ladled into
A hand-thrown pottery bowl

Hot rye bread
On a wooden
Cutting board

The drifting
Scent of fresh
Banana cake

The spatter of sparks
Shooting out
Against the fireplace screen

A stack of unread library books

All tucked in
By driven
White crystals.

— Sheryl L. Nelms

Cookies Galore

■ Cookies Galore ■

Dr. Pepper Snowballs 37
Pink Frosted Cookies 37
Frosted Jam Bars 38
Disappearing Marshmallow Bars 38
Soft Date Bars 39
Orange-Nut Balls 39
Oatmeal Cookie Mix 40
True Goodie Bars 40
Praline Cookies 41
Coconut Crisps 41
Peanut Butter Middles 42
Zucchini Bars 42
Cherub Coins 43
Mincemeat Drop Cookies 43
Butterscotch Cheesecake Bars 44
'Cowless' Cow Patties 44
Cowboy Cookies 45
Coconut Macaroon Cookies 45
Jumbo Cookies 46
Chelsea's Choco-Nutty Crunch Bars 47
Roll 'n' Cut Cookies 48
York Brownies 48
Magic Peanut Butter Cookies 49
Monster Cookies 50
Cranberry Cheesecake Bars 50
Gourmet Cookies 51
Chocolate Crispy Bars 51
Oatmeal Fruit Cookies 52
Pineapple-Oatmeal Drops 52
Double Chocolate Crumble Bars 53
Cherry Chip Brownies 53
Chocolate Malt Ball Cookies 54
Oatmeal Lemon-Cheese Cookies 55
Hanukkah Gelt Cookies 56

Dr. Pepper Snowballs

This is a no-bake treat.

3½ cups vanilla wafer crumbs (1 box)
¼ cup margarine, melted
¾ cup powdered sugar, sifted
1 cup pecans, chopped
½ cup Dr. Pepper soft drink

Icing:
2 cups powdered sugar, sifted
2 Tbsps. margarine, melted
⅓ cup Dr. Pepper soft drink
¼ tsp. vanilla
1 pkg. flaked coconut

Mix crumbs, margarine, sifted powdered sugar, pecans and Dr. Pepper. Roll into very small balls.

To make icing, measure sifted powdered sugar into mixing bowl. Add melted margarine, Dr. Pepper and vanilla. Using a fork, dip balls In icing then roll in flaked coconut. Makes 6 dozen.

Ethel Williams
Lawrenceville, Pennsylvania
February 12, 1991

Pink Frosted Cookies

These are pretty to make for holidays.

2¼ cups sifted flour
½ cup granulated sugar
1 cup softened butter
2 eggs
1 cup brown sugar
½ tsp. salt
½ tsp. baking powder
½ tsp. vanilla
1 2-oz. jar maraschino cherries, drained and chopped (reserve juice)
½ cup walnuts
½ cup flaked coconut
1 Tbsp. butter
1 cup powdered sugar

Mix flour, granulated sugar and butter until crumbly. Press into 9x13x2-inch pan and bake 20 minutes in 350° oven.

Blend eggs, brown sugar, salt, baking powder and vanilla. Add cherries, walnuts and coconut. Place on top of baked crust and bake 20 minutes.

Combine butter and powdered sugar, adding enough juice from cherries to be of spreading consistency. Spread on top of baked layers and sprinkle with coconut. When cool, cut into squares.

Mrs. Beryl Swan
Kansas City, Missouri
November 29, 1985

Frosted Jam Bars

These will be gone before you get them out of the pan!

½ cup butter OR margarine
½ cup dark corn syrup
1 beaten egg
½ tsp. vanilla
1½ cups sifted flour
1 tsp. baking powder
½ tsp. salt
½ tsp. cinnamon
¾ cup jam OR preserves (Strawberry is great.)

Melt butter or margarine, stir in dark corn syrup. Mix in egg and vanilla. Add dry ingredients and mix well. Spread half of batter in greased 7x11x1½-inch pan. Spoon jam or preserves over batter; carefully cover with remaining batter. Bake in 400° oven for 20-25 minutes. Frost while warm with powdered sugar icing. Cool. Cut into bars.

Nancy Gallivan
David L. Gallivan
Halfway, Missouri
March 21, 1972

Disappearing Marshmallow Bars

½ cup butterscotch bits
¼ cup butter OR margarine
¾ cup flour
⅓ cup brown sugar
1 tsp. baking powder
¼ tsp. salt
½ tsp. vanilla
½ tsp. burnt sugar extract
1 egg
1 cup miniature marshmallows
1 cup chocolate bits
⅓ cup chopped nuts

Melt butterscotch bits and butter in heavy saucepan, stirring constantly. Cool and add flour, brown sugar, baking powder, salt, flavorings and egg. Mix well. Fold in marshmallows, chocolate bits and nuts. Spread into a greased 9-inch square pan. Bake in 350° oven for 20-25 minutes.

Do not overbake. Center will be jiggly, but becomes firm with cooling.

Mrs. Sandford Wickham
Holbrook, Nebraska
January 15, 1985

Soft Date Bars

These would be nice to serve on Christmas Day or at a party.

2 cups chopped dates
⅓ cup boiling water
½ cup shortening
1 cup granulated sugar
¾ tsp. salt
2 eggs, beaten
1 tsp. vanilla extract
1 cup flour
¼ tsp. baking soda
½ cup nuts
• powdered sugar

Pour the boiling water over dates and let stand until cool. Cream together the shortening and granulated sugar. Add salt, eggs and vanilla. Add date mixture and blend. Add flour sifted with baking soda. Then add nuts. Spread in a large, greased 9x13-inch pan. Bake in 350° oven for 40 minutes. Cool in pan. Cut bars and roll in powdered sugar.

Mae Wicht
Yutan, Nebraska
December 4, 1990

Orange-Nut Balls

These simple and flavorful balls may be frozen until needed.

1½ cup crushed vanilla wafers
1 cup powdered sugar
¼ cup melted margarine
1 cup finely chopped pecans
¼ cup undiluted frozen orange juice

Combine wafer crumbs, powdered sugar, margarine and pecans. Add orange juice and mix thoroughly. Form into small balls. Roll in powdered sugar, nuts or coconut. Freeze until needed.

Mildred Sherrer
Bay City, Texas
October 11, 1994

■ Cookie Jar Heroine ■

The little hand
raised the ceramic lid
and rescued
the last cookie
from the dungeon of the cookie jar

— Harley Palmer

Oatmeal Cookie Mix

This is so convenient to have on hand.

6 cups quick-cooking OR old-fashioned oatmeal
4 cups flour
2 cups granulated sugar
2 cups brown sugar
2 tsps. salt
2 tsps. baking powder
1 tsp. baking soda
1 cup butter OR margarine
1 cup shortening

In a very large bowl, stir together first 7 ingredients. With pastry blender, put in butter and shortening until fine crumbs form. Refrigerate mix in airtight container. Makes 16 cups.

To make cookies, stir container of mix then measure 4 cups. Add ⅔ cup raisins, 2 eggs and 1 teaspoon vanilla. Mix until blended. Drop dough by heaping teaspoons, 3 inches apart, on greased baking sheet. Bake in 350° oven for 10-12 minutes. Makes 32 cookies.

Salome Schmucker
Medford, Wisconsin
September 26, 1989

True Goodie Bars

This is my brother's favorite cookie recipe. I only make it for Christmas and special occasions since it takes a little extra work.

1 12-oz. pkg. chocolate chips
1 12-oz. pkg. butterscotch chips
1 18-oz. jar peanut butter
1 cup butter OR margarine
½ cup milk
1 3-oz. pkg. instant vanilla pudding
2 lbs. powdered sugar
½ tsp. maple flavoring
1 lb. dry roasted peanuts

Melt together chocolate chips, butterscotch chips and peanut butter. Spread half of this mixture in a jelly-roll pan and refrigerate. Boil together butter, milk and vanilla pudding. Add powdered sugar and flavoring. Beat by hand and spread over chilled mixture. To other half of chocolate chip mixture add peanuts. Pour over first half and refrigerate. Cut into bars.

Lessie L. Russell
Seattle, Washington
November 8, 1994

Praline Cookies

⅔ cup shortening
1 cup granulated sugar
½ cup molasses
2 eggs
½ tsp. vanilla flavoring
1 tsp. burnt sugar flavoring
1¾ cups flour
½ tsp. baking soda
¼ tsp. mace
¼ tsp. salt
1½-2 cups nutmeats

Slowly melt shortening and cool. Add granulated sugar and molasses, mixing well. Add eggs and flavorings; beat well. Sift together flour, soda, mace and salt. Add to first mixture. Add nutmeats and drop by scant teaspoonful onto greased and floured baking sheet, 2 inches apart. Bake in 375° oven for 8-10 minutes. Remove from pan immediately. This makes about 8 dozen cookies.

Mrs. O. Petersen
Utica, South Dakota
October 24, 1989

Coconut Crisps

2 cups sifted flour
½ tsp. baking powder
½ tsp. baking soda
½ cup butter OR margarine
1½ cups granulated sugar
2 eggs
½ tsp. orange extract
½ tsp. vanilla
1 Tbsp. milk
½ cup finely chopped pecans
2 cups flaked coconut

Sift flour with baking powder and baking soda. Cream butter or margarine; gradually add granulated sugar and cream until light and fluffy. Add eggs and flavorings and beat well; then add flour mixture. Add milk and blend well. Add pecans and coconut.
Drop from teaspoon onto greased baking sheets. Bake at 375° for 10-12 minutes or until lightly browned.

Joan Nesmith
Williams, Minnesota
January 4, 1994

CHARMING COOKIE EXCHANGES

A cookie exchange charms everyone. Each guest brings one or two plates, tins or baskets of their favorite treat, along with the recipe, to exchange with another guest for their sweet treat. As host or hostess, serve several of your favorite cakes and cookies, along with hot chocolate, apple cider or egg nog.

To put guests in a "Christmas cookie" mood even before the exchange, put your creativity to use shaping and writing the invitation like a recipe card. The ingredients are: good friends, sweet treats and holiday cheer.

Peanut Butter Middles

This cookie is a favorite of my grandchildren and a big hit at Vacation Bible School.

1½ cups flour
½ cup cocoa
½ tsp. soda
½ cup granulated sugar
½ cup brown sugar
½ cup margarine, softened
¼ cup peanut butter
1 egg
1 tsp. vanilla

Filling:
1 cup peanut butter
1 cup powdered sugar

Combine flour, cocoa and soda and set aside. Beat together brown and granulated sugars, margarine, peanut butter, egg and vanilla. Add flour mixture. Form mixture into 40 balls.

For filling, blend peanut butter and powdered sugar and form into 40 balls. Wrap the chocolate mixture balls around the filling mixture balls and place on ungreased baking sheet. Flatten with a glass dipped in granulated sugar. Bake at 375° for 7-9 minutes or until slightly cracked.

Mrs. Evelyn Myers
Geneva, Nebraska
July 5, 1994

Zucchini Bars

Super bar cookies to try!

Cookies:
2 cups granulated sugar
1 cup salad oil
2 eggs
2½ cups flour
1 tsp. soda
1 tsp. salt
1 tsp. baking powder
1 tsp. cinnamon
3 cups grated zucchini
½ cup nuts
1 cup chocolate bits

Frosting:
4 Tbsps. margarine
1 3-oz. pkg. cream cheese
1 tsp. vanilla
1½ cups powdered sugar

Beat granulated sugar, oil and eggs together by hand. Add flour, soda, salt, baking powder, cinnamon, zucchini and nuts. Pour into greased jelly-roll pan. Sprinkle with chocolate bits. Bake for 40 minutes at 350°, checking after 30 minutes for doneness. Cool. Combine margarine, cream cheese, vanilla and powdered sugar, mixing well; frost.

Rose Ann Miller
Rudd, Iowa
August 16, 1994

Cherub Coins

These are great-tasting cookies.

¾   cup butter OR margarine
1½   cups firmly packed light brown sugar
1   egg, unbeaten
2   cups sifted cake flour
⅛   tsp. baking soda
½   tsp. salt
¼   cup finely chopped pecans

Cream butter or margarine and brown sugar, add egg and mix well. Sift flour, baking soda and salt together and add gradually to egg mixture, stirring after each addition. Stir in chopped pecans and chill overnight.

Shape into tiny balls ½ inch in diameter. Place on greased cookie sheets; flatten slightly with thumbs. Bake at 375° for 8-10 minutes. Let stand a few minutes before removing from cookie sheet. Makes about 10 dozen cookies.

Mrs. A. Mayer
Richmond, Virginia
December 17, 1991

Mincemeat Drop Cookies

This makes a very moist cookie.

3¼   cups sifted all-purpose flour
½   tsp. salt
1   tsp. soda
1   tsp. cinnamon
1   cup soft shortening OR margarine
1   cup granulated sugar
½   cup brown sugar, packed
3   eggs, unbeaten
1   tsp. vanilla
1½   cups prepared mincemeat
1   cup raisins
1   cup chopped nuts, optional

Preheat oven to 375°. Sift together flour, salt, soda and cinnamon. Combine shortening or margarine, sugars, eggs and vanilla in mixing bowl. Cream on "beat-whip" speed for 2 minutes. Stop, scrape bowl. Add mincemeat and ½ cup flour mixture. Blend in on "fold-blend" setting, then on "beat-whip" for ½ minute. Add remaining flour and repeat. Stop, scrape bowl, beat in raisins and nuts.

Drop by scant teaspoonfuls on greased cookie sheet. Bake about 10 minutes in preheated oven. Remove from oven and cool on wire rack. When cold, store in air-tight container. Makes about 10 dozen cookies.

Mrs. L.W. Mayer
Richmond, Virginia
January 2, 1990

Butterscotch Cheesecake Bars

These are very good.

1   12-oz. pkg. butterscotch morsels
⅓   cup margarine
2   cups graham cracker crumbs
1   cup chopped nuts
1   8-oz. pkg. cream cheese, softened
1   14-oz. can sweetened condensed milk
1   tsp. vanilla extract
1   egg

Preheat oven to 350° (325° if using glass dish). In medium saucepan, melt morsels and margarine; stir in crumbs and nuts. Press half the mixture firmly onto the bottom of a greased 9x13-inch pan.

In large mixer bowl, beat cheese until fluffy. Beat in condensed milk, vanilla and egg. Mix well. Pour into prepared pan and top with remaining crumb mixture. Bake 25-30 minutes or until toothpick inserted near center comes out clean. Cool to room temperature. Chill before cutting into bars. Refrigerate leftovers.

Bernice Knutson
Soldier, Iowa
July 19, 1994

'Cowless' Cow Patties

This is a very good cookie with an unusual name.

1   cup shortening
1   cup margarine
2   cups granulated sugar
2   cups brown sugar
4   eggs
2   tsps. vanilla
1   tsp. baking soda
1   tsp. baking powder
4   cups flour
1   cup shredded coconut
1   cup pecan pieces
2   cups corn flakes
1   6-oz. pkg. chocolate chips

Cream shortening, margarine and sugars. Add beaten eggs and vanilla. Add flour, baking powder and soda, mixing well. Add nuts, coconut, chocolate chips and corn flakes. Mix and drop by large spoonfuls on cookie sheet. Spread each 1 slightly with back of spoon. Bake 15 minutes or more in 350° oven.

Mrs. Irey Knoll
Osborne, Kansas
June 18, 1991

Cowboy Cookies

1 cup butter OR margarine
½ cup granulated sugar
1½ cups brown sugar
2 eggs
2 cups flour
1 tsp. baking soda
½ tsp. salt
1½ tsps. vanilla
2 cups rolled oats, uncooked
1 cup flaked coconut OR raisins
1 12-oz. pkg. chocolate chips

Cream butter and sugars. Add eggs and beat well. Mix in remaining ingredients. Drop by teaspoonfuls onto a greased cookie sheet and bake at 350° for about 15 minutes.

Ardis Jensen
Lincoln, Kansas
August 15, 1989

Coconut Macaroon Cookies

This is a large recipe and very good.

4 egg whites
2 cups granulated sugar
¼ tsp. salt
• vanilla to taste
2 cups coconut
4 cups corn flakes

Beat egg whites until stiff. Gradually add granulated sugar and salt, beating well. Add vanilla and fold in coconut and corn flakes. Drop from teaspoon onto greased cookie sheet. Bake in 350° oven for 10-12 minutes.

Mrs. D. Hardgrove
Fort Dodge, Iowa
May 13, 1986

■ Granny's Sugar Bowl ■

*It's not made of cut glass,
It lacks elegance and grace,
But when I look at it,
I see Granny's loving face.
She gave it for a gift,
On the day we were wed,
And when I fill it,
I remember what she said,
"Sugar makes the tea sweet
And the coffee too,
Sweet words sweeten life,
When spoken kind and true."*

— Ruth Owens

Jumbo Cookies

Have you ever been in a bakery when one of the bakers brought out a cookie that could serve as dessert for a family of 12? I always wondered if they had little elves in the kitchen that helped them make jumbo cookies.

½ **cup margarine OR butter**
¾ **cup packed dark OR light brown sugar**
3 **Tbsps. granulated sugar**
1½ **tsps. vanilla extract**
1 **large egg**
1½ **cups all-purpose flour**
½ **tsp. salt**
¾ **tsp. baking soda**
1-1½ **cups semi-sweet chocolate chips OR 1 or more of your favorite ingredients**

At medium speed in a large bowl, beat the margarine or butter with brown sugar. Add granulated sugar and beat until creamy. Blend in vanilla and egg. At low speed, blend in flour, salt and soda. Stir in 1 cup of chocolate chips, chopped nuts, M&M's, coconut, or any combination you desire. Set aside an additional ½ cup of the same ingredient for sprinkling on top later. Chill dough in refrigerator for about 1½ hours or in the freezer for about 45 minutes. Grease 12x½-inch deep round foil baking pan or 12-inch round pizza pan. Place dough in pan and press it evenly within 1½ inches of the edge. Sprinkle reserved topping on dough.

Bake in 325° oven for 30-35 minutes or until edges are lightly browned. Cool on rack, then remove from pan. To store, wrap in plastic wrap, then in foil.

This cookie is fun to give on holidays and birthdays. A good way to let someone know how much you care.

Mildred Hyink
Muscatine, Iowa
January 2, 1990

BEST COOKIE BAKING TIPS
To ensure uniform baking, make all of the cookies in 1 batch the same size and shape, according to the measurement specified in each recipe. Shiny, heavy-gauge aluminum cookie sheets promote uniform browning. Always place dough on cool cookie sheets. Otherwise, dough will spread before it's in the oven, resulting in improperly baked and irregularly shaped cookies. Evenly space cookies on the cookie sheet for even baking. Use flat cookie sheets with low edges so air can circulate over the cookies.

Preheat the oven for 15 minutes before baking. Check at the end of the minimum baking time to determine doneness—baking times can

Chelsea's Choco-Nutty Crunch Bars

1¼ cups all-purpose flour
1 cup powdered sugar
½ cup cocoa
1 cup margarine
1 13½-oz. can evaporated milk
1 egg, beaten
2 tsps. vanilla
1½ cups chopped M&M's OR other chocolate-covered peanut candy

Fudge Frosting:
2½ cups powdered sugar, sifted
¼ cup cocoa
¼ cup corn oil margarine
3 Tbsps. boiling water
½ tsp. vanilla

Preheat oven to 350°. In large bowl, combine flour, powdered sugar and cocoa; cut in margarine until crumbly. Press firmly on bottom of lightly greased 9x13-inch baking pan. Bake 15 minutes.

In medium bowl, combine evaporated milk, egg and vanilla; mix well. Stir in chopped candy. Spread evenly over baked crust. Bake 25 minutes or until lightly browned. Cool. Frost with Fudge Frosting. Cut into bars and store in refrigerator. Makes 3 dozen.

To make frosting: In a medium mixing bowl, combine powdered sugar and cocoa. Add margarine, boiling water and vanilla. Beat on low speed until well blended and smooth. Beat 1 minute on medium speed. Cool and frost.

Christine Gibson
Evansville, Indiana
September 29, 1992

---

vary depending upon the oven. Follow the test for doneness in each recipe. Use large eggs in recipes unless otherwise specified.

Remove cookies from cookie sheets as soon as they are rigid enough to transfer to cooling racks. Recipes will indicate whether cookies need to be removed immediately or cooled for a few minutes prior to removing from the sheet. Cookies should be cooled on cooling racks with enough space around them to allow air to circulate. Cool bar cookies in the pan set on the rack.

■ STORING COOKIES

Store cookies in airtight containers. Cool completely first or they will release steam and become soggy.

Store only 1 kind of cookie per container. Moist cookies packed with crisp ones can cause the crisp ones to soften.

Store different flavors of cookies in separate containers. Soft, cake-like, frosted or decorated cookies should be stored with waxed paper between layers to protect them. If bar cookies are to be eaten immediately, they may be stored in the baking pan. Keep tightly covered.

Roll 'n' Cut Cookies

Lactose-intolerant people can enjoy this recipe. For each cup of butter in a recipe, use 1 cup of butter-flavored shortening, plus 1-2 tablespoons of water.

1 cup butter-flavored shortening
1 cup granulated sugar
1 large egg, PLUS 2 Tbsps. water
½ tsp. vanilla
2¾ cups flour
½ tsp. baking soda

Beat shortening and granulated sugar until light and fluffy. Beat in egg, water and vanilla. Add remaining ingredients and mix well. Form dough into a ball.

Roll ⅓ dough on floured surface to ¼-inch thickness. Cut out shapes and place on greased cookie sheet. Bake in preheated 325° oven 10-15 minutes. Use the same method for remaining dough.

Cynthia E. Georgeff
Lutz, Florida
April 27, 1993

York Brownies

This is very rich and could be served with vanilla ice cream or whipped topping to make a nice-looking dessert.

1½ cups butter OR margarine (3 sticks), melted
3 cups granulated sugar
1 Tbsp. vanilla
5 eggs
2 cups flour
1 cup cocoa
1 tsp. baking powder
1 tsp. salt
24 small (1½-inch-diameter) chocolate-covered peppermint patties, unwrapped

Grease 9x13x2-inch baking pan. In a large bowl, stir together butter, granulated sugar and vanilla. Add eggs; stir until well blended. Stir in flour, cocoa, baking powder and salt; blend well. Reserve 2 cups of batter; set aside. Spread remaining batter in prepared pan. Arrange peppermints patties in single layer over batter, about ½-inch apart. Spread reserved 2 cups batter over the patties. Bake at 350° (325° for glass pan) 50-55 minutes or until brownies begin to pull away from sides of pan. Cool completely in pan. Cut into squares. Makes 36 brownies.

June Formanek
Belle Plaine, Iowa
April 26, 1994

Magic Peanut Butter Cookies

This cookie has a surprise when you bite into it. Kids love them.

Dough:
- 1½ cups flour
- ½ cup cocoa
- ½ tsp. baking soda
- ½ cup granulated sugar
- ½ cup brown sugar, packed
- ½ cup margarine, softened
- ¼ cup peanut butter
- 1 tsp. vanilla
- 1 egg

Filling:
- ¾ cup peanut butter
- ¾ cup powdered sugar

Combine flour, cocoa and soda in a small bowl. In a large bowl, beat granulated sugar, brown sugar, margarine and peanut butter until light and fluffy. Add vanilla and egg, beating well. Add flour mixture.

In a small bowl, combine filling ingredients and blend. Roll into 30 small (1-inch) balls.

For each cookie, shape, with floured hands, 1 tablespoon dough around 1 peanut butter ball, covering completely. Place 2 inches apart on ungreased cookie sheet. Flatten with bottom of a glass dipped in granulated sugar. Bake in 375° oven for 7-9 minutes or until set and slightly cracked. Cool. Decorate if desired. Makes 30 cookies.

June Formanek
Belle Plaine, Iowa
December 8, 1992

■ Companionship ■

My recipe book
is thumbed and tattered.
Pages are sticky.
Some are splattered.

Through constant use
it's become a friend.
May our togetherness
never end.

— Claire Puneky

Monster Cookies

This recipe does not call for any flour or baking powder.

1 dozen eggs
1 lb. butter OR margarine
2 lbs. brown sugar
4 cups granulated sugar
¼ cup vanilla
3 lbs. peanut butter
8 tsps. baking soda
18 cups quick oatmeal
1 lb. chocolate chips
1 lb. chopped nuts
1 lb. golden raisins

Mix the eggs, butter, brown sugar, granulated sugar and vanilla in a very large bowl. This will need lots of stirring. Add peanut butter and mix well. Add soda, oatmeal and chopped nuts. Stir in chocolate chips and raisins.

Shape into balls and flatten on greased cookie sheet. (I don't flatten the balls.) Bake in 350° oven for 10-12 minutes. (I bake them 8 minutes.) Do not let them get too large.

This recipe can be cut down to smaller quantities very easily. They store and freeze well for future use.

Tammy Dodson
Topeka, Kansas
October 27, 1992

Cranberry Cheesecake Bars

These would be good for the holidays.

1 pkg. butter recipe cake mix
½ cup margarine OR butter, softened
1 egg
¼ cup chopped pecans
1 8-oz. pkg. cream cheese, softened
¼ cup powdered sugar
½ tsp. vanilla
1 tsp. almond extract
1 egg
1 16-oz. can whole berry cranberry sauce
¼ tsp. nutmeg

Mix together cake mix, margarine, 1 egg and pecans. Press into the bottom of a greased and floured 9x13-inch baking pan. Bake at 350° for 5-8 minutes. Remove from oven.

In a bowl, combine cream cheese, powdered sugar, vanilla and almond extracts and 1 egg. Pour over crust. Add nutmeg to cranberry sauce and spoon over cream cheese to form swirls. Bake at 350° for 30-40 minutes. Cut into bars. Makes 15 or 16 bars.

Rose M. Dietz
Hoisington, Kansas
November 19, 1991

Gourmet Cookies

These cookies are delicious!

1 cup, PLUS 2 Tbsps. margarine
1½ cups granulated sugar
¾ cup light brown sugar
1½ tsps. vanilla
3 eggs
4½ cups flour
1½ tsps. baking soda
3 cups pecans
10 ozs. milk chocolate chunks
10 ozs. white chocolate chunks

In large bowl, combine margarine, sugars and vanilla. Add eggs, beating well. Combine flour and baking soda, blending into creamed mixture. Stir in nuts and chocolate chunks. Drop on ungreased cookie sheets. Bake in 350° oven 10-12 minutes.

Esther Denish
Monroe City, Missouri
October 22, 1991

Chocolate Crispy Bars

My grandchildren all love these.

1 cup granulated sugar
1 cup corn syrup
1 cup peanut butter
6 cups crispy rice cereal
1 6-oz. pkg. milk chocolate chips
1 6-oz. pkg. regular chocolate chips

Bring granulated sugar and corn syrup to a boil in a 3-quart pan. Remove from heat. Add peanut butter, mixing well. Add rice cereal. Press mixture into a buttered 9x13x2-inch pan. Melt chips together over hot (not boiling) water. Spread over cereal mixture in pan. Chill until top is firm. Cut into bars.

Dorothy Bunch
Lebanon, Oregon
December 22, 1992

SHIPPING COOKIES

Bar, drop and fruit cookies can best withstand mailing. Tender, fragile cookies are apt to crumble when shipped.

When shipping baked goods, use a heavy cardboard box or empty coffee can lined with aluminum foil or plastic food wrap. Wrap 4 to 6 cookies of the same size in foil, plastic wrap or plastic food bags; seal securely with freezer tape. Place the heaviest cookies in container bottom and layer wrapped cookies with crumpled paper towel around them. Seal container with freezer, plastic or adhesive tape. Wrap the container with an outer paper wrapper. Lastly, mark the package "PERISHABLE FOOD" to ensure more rapid transit and careful handling.

Oatmeal Fruit Cookies

This is an excellent recipe for people with diabetes.

1   cup sifted flour
1   tsp. baking soda
1   cup water
½   cup chopped, pitted dates
½   cup peeled and chopped apples
½   cup raisins
½   cup margarine OR butter
1   cup quick-cooking oatmeal
2   eggs, beaten
1   tsp. vanilla
½   cup chopped walnuts

Sift flour and baking soda together. Set aside. Over medium-high heat, bring water, dates, apples and raisins to a boil. Reduce heat to low; simmer 3 minutes. Remove from heat. Add margarine; stir until melted. Pour into large bowl; cool slightly. Stir in dry ingredients, oatmeal, beaten eggs, vanilla and chopped walnuts until well blended. Cover and refrigerate overnight. Drop by heaping teaspoons, 2 inches apart, on greased cookie sheets. Bake in 350° oven 12-14 minutes. Cool on racks. Store in refrigerator in airtight container.

Joan Calkins
Aurora, Nebraska
November 5, 1991

Pineapple Oatmeal Drops

This cookie is so moist and delicately flavored.

½   cup shortening, butter OR margarine
1   cup granulated sugar
¼   tsp. cinnamon
⅛   tsp. nutmeg
1   egg, unbeaten
1   cup (8 ozs.) crushed pineapple undrained (if too much juice, add more flour OR oatmeal)
1   cup flour
½   tsp. salt
½   tsp. soda
1½   cups quick oatmeal
½   cup chopped nuts

Cream margarine, granulated sugar and spices until fluffy. Beat in egg and stir in the pineapple. Sift flour with salt and soda and add to mixture. Add oatmeal and nuts, mixing well. Drop by spoonful on greased baking sheets. Bake in 375° oven for 12-15 minutes. Cool a minute and remove from baking sheet. Makes about 4 dozen.

Marian Choquet
Sterling, Colorado
July 18, 1989

Double Chocolate Crumble Bars

These are scrumptious!

½ cup margarine
¾ cup granulated sugar
2 eggs
1 tsp. vanilla
¾ cup flour
2 Tbsps. cocoa
¼ tsp. baking powder
½ cup nuts, optional
2 cups miniature marshmallows
1 6-oz. pkg. chocolate chips
1 cup peanut butter
1½ cups crispy rice cereal

Cream together margarine and granulated sugar. Add eggs and vanilla, mixing well. Add flour, cocoa, baking powder and nuts. Spread on greased 9x13-inch pan and bake in 350° oven for 15 minutes. Remove from oven and sprinkle marshmallows over top. Return to oven for 3 minutes. In large saucepan, melt chocolate chips with peanut butter. Add crisp rice cereal and spread over top of baked mixture. Refrigerate or put in very cool place. Cut into bars.

Avis Bristol
Waco, Nebraska
November 11, 1986

Cherry Chip Brownies

The creamy chocolate frosting makes these brownies extra good.

1 21-oz. can cherry pie filling
1 18.5-oz. pkg. chocolate cake mix
2 eggs, beaten
1 tsp. almond extract
1 cup granulated sugar
⅓ cup evaporated milk
5 Tbsps. butter OR margarine
1 6-oz. pkg. semi-sweet chocolate chips

Preheat oven to 350°. Combine pie filling, cake mix, eggs and almond extract in a large bowl. Mix until well blended. Spread mixture into a lightly greased and floured 10½x15½-inch jelly-roll pan. Bake for 20-25 minutes or until done. Cool.
Combine granulated sugar, milk and butter or margarine in a small saucepan. Mix well. Bring to a boil and boil for 1 minute. Remove from heat. Add chocolate chips. Stir until melted. Spread over cooled brownies. Cool completely and cut into bars.

Bobbie Mae Cooley
Bowen, Illinois
March 1, 1994

Chocolate Malt Ball Cookies

¾ cup brown sugar
1 tsp. vanilla
1⅓ sticks margarine OR vegetable shortening
1 egg
1¾ cups all-purpose flour
⅓ cup cocoa
½ tsp. salt (if desired and shortening is used)
½ cup malted milk powder (NOT chocolate)
¾ tsp. baking soda
2 cups malted milk balls, crushed (to crush, put candy in sealable plastic bag and pound with rolling pin or a heavy spoon)

Beat together brown sugar, vanilla and margarine in large bowl until mixed; beat in egg and mix well. Mix together flour, cocoa, salt, malted milk powder and baking soda. Add to creamed mixture and mix until blended. Stir in malted milk ball pieces. Drop on ungreased cookie sheet by rounded tablespoonfuls 2 inches apart. Bake 1 sheet at a time at 375° for 7-9 minutes or until cookies are set. Do not overbake. Cool 2 minutes before removing to sheets of foil to cool completely. Makes about 3 dozen cookies.

Hazel Johnson
Wymore, Nebraska
October 11, 1994

■ Baking in the Third Generation ■

Rolling out my cookie dough
with Grandma's rolling pin,
I marvel at this hunk of wood,
and ponder where it's been.

From a maple bedpost long ago,
my grandma carved each end
to grasp while rolling out her dough —
she knew well how to fend.

Her sugar cookies, fluted, round,
the best I've ever tasted,
were crisper than my recipe
and not a crumb was wasted.

Oatmeal Lemon-Cheese Cookies

1 cup buttery flavored shortening
1 3-oz. pkg. cream cheese, softened
1¼ cups granulated sugar
1 egg, separated
1 tsp. lemon extract
2 tsps. grated lemon peel
1¼ cups all-purpose flour
1¼ cups quick OR old-fashioned oatmeal, uncooked
½ tsp. salt
1 egg
• granulated sugar
½ cup sliced almonds

Heat oven to 350°. Combine shortening, cream cheese and 1¼ cups granulated sugar in large bowl. Beat at medium speed of electric mixer until well blended. Beat in egg yolk, lemon extract and lemon peel.

Combine flour, oats and salt. Stir into creamed mixture with spoon until blended.

Drop rounded measuring teaspoonfuls of dough 2 inches apart onto ungreased baking sheet. Beat whole egg with reserved egg white. Brush over tops of cookies. Sprinkle lightly with granulated sugar. Press almond slices lightly on top. Bake at 350° for 10-12 minutes, or until edges are lightly browned. Cool 2 minutes on baking sheet before removing to cooling rack. Makes 6 dozen.

**Kate Marchbanks Food Story
September 29, 1992**

With this pin, my mother rolled
her pies and biscuit dough.
I've used it more than forty years
while helping children grow —

Many a cookie Santa Claus
I've rolled out with this pin
for daughters, now called "Grandma" too,
(A thought that makes me grin)!

And when the days grow short for me,
some daughter will inherit
my grandma's maple rolling pin,
but not yet — I can't spare it!

— Joyce McDavid Douglas

Hanukkah Gelt Cookies

1½   **cups firmly packed light brown sugar**
⅔   **cup all-vegetable shortening**
1   **Tbsp. water**
1   **tsp. vanilla**
2   **eggs**
1½   **cups all-purpose flour**
⅓   **cup unsweetened baking cocoa powder**
¼   **tsp. baking soda**
½   **tsp. salt**
2   **cups (12-oz. pkg.) semi-sweet chocolate chips**

Preheat oven to 375°. Place sheets of foil on countertop for cooling cookies. Combine brown sugar, shortening, water and vanilla in large bowl. Beat at medium speed of electric mixer until well blended. Beat eggs into creamed mixture. Combine flour, cocoa powder, baking soda and salt. Mix into creamed mixture at low speed just until blended. Stir in chocolate chips. Drop rounded tablespoonfuls of dough 2 inches apart onto ungreased baking sheet. Bake 1 baking sheet at a time, 7-9 minutes, or until cookies are set. Do not overbake. Cool 2 minutes on baking sheet. Remove cookies to foil to cool completely. Makes about 3 dozen cookies.

Kate Marchbanks Food Story
December 7, 1993

COOKIE BASKETS FULL OF CHEER

To spread some sweetness within your community, share delicious delights with a local nursing home, retirement community, school or hospital. Turn your kitchen into a cookie workshop and spend a Saturday afternoon baking an assortment of cookies with your family. Then fill gift baskets, tins or even decorated brown paper lunch bags with your cookie creations and attach gift tags wishing the unsuspecting receivers "Happy Holidays!"

Delivering "cookie baskets full of cheer" is a fun family event that can become a tradition in the spirit of the season.

Savory
Main Dishes

■ Savory Main Dishes ■

Reuben Pie 59
Impossible Taco Pie 59
Shepherd's Pie 60
Swedish Meatballs 60
Spaghetti and Meatballs, Family Style 61
Marvelous Meatballs 62
Beans and Meatballs 62
Hearty Swirled Meat Loaf with Cheese 63
Super Meat Loaf 64
Horseradish Beef Pot Roast 64
Pepsi Pork Roast 65
Lasagne 65
Crafty Crescent Lasagne 66
Zucchini Beef Casserole 67
Poor Man's Steak 67
Restaurant Chili 68
Crock Pizza 69
Easy Microwave Pizza Breads 69
Cranberry and Bean Casserole 70
Sweet Barbecue Pork Chops 70
Sausage Apple Bean Bake 71
Cheese and Sausage Bake 71
Manicotti 72
Scrapple 73
Good Morning Casserole 73
Cheese and Potato Wild Rice Soup 74
Monterey Pizza Rice 74
Best-Ever Turkey Casserole 75
Yum-Yum Casserole 75
Baked Chicken Puff 76
Chicken Breasts with Asparagus 76
Oven Barbecued Chicken 77
Baked Chicken Breasts with Cranberry Sauce 77
Chicken Dressing Casserole 78
Chicken Breasts, Picnic Style 78
Quick Low-Fat Raspberry Chicken .79
Chicken Pot Pie 79
Kathie's Artichoke Bake 80
Tuna Rolls 81
Seafood Enchiladas 82
Tuna Burgers 82
Veggie Pizza 83

Reuben Pie

Here's a nice fall recipe to tempt the family.

5   slices rye bread, crusts removed
2   Tbsps. mustard
1   cup Swiss cheese, shredded
1   cup corned beef, chopped
¾   cup sauerkraut
2   eggs, beaten
¾   cup milk

Press bread slices around greased pie pan. Spread mustard over bread. Place cheese, corned beef and sauerkraut on top.

In medium bowl, combine eggs and milk. Beat well. Pour egg mixture over pie. Bake in preheated 325° oven for 40 minutes. Makes 6 servings.

Louise Mayer
Richmond, Virginia
October 12, 1993

Impossible Taco Pie

I think you will like this.

1   lb. ground beef
½   cup onion, chopped
1   1½-oz. envelope taco sauce mix
1¼   cups milk
3   eggs
¾   cup biscuit mix
1   cup shredded Monterey Jack OR Cheddar cheese
1   4-oz. can chopped green chilies, drained
2   tomatoes, sliced

Heat oven to 400°. Grease a 10-inch pie pan. Brown beef and onions in skillet about 10 minutes and drain. Stir in taco mix. Spread in pie pan. Beat milk, biscuit mix and eggs until smooth (15 seconds in a blender on high or 1 minute with a hand beater). Pour over meat mixture. Bake 25 minutes and top with chilies, tomatoes and cheese. Bake 8-10 minutes longer or until knife inserted in center comes out clean. Cool 5 minutes. Serve with sour cream, chopped tomatoes, shredded lettuce and shredded cheese, if desired. Makes 6-8 servings.

Marion Armstrong
Alma, Kansas
April 11, 1989

Shepherd's Pie

Think of the herdsmen tending their sheep and goats, and celebrate Christmas by trying this pie.

1 prepared pie shell, unbaked
1 lb. lean ground beef
3 medium onions, sliced
1 4-oz. can mushroom pieces and stems with liquid
1 tsp. salt
1 Tbsp. Worcestershire sauce
1 beef bouillon cube, dissolved in 1 cup hot water
2 Tbsps. flour, mixed with a little of the bouillon
2 cups biscuit mix
1 cup milk
1 cup sour cream
½ cup shredded Cheddar cheese

Brown the onions and meat. Add mushrooms, salt, Worcestershire sauce, bouillon and flour. Blend well and bring to a gentle boil in saucepan for 5 minutes. Turn mixture into unbaked pie shell.

Combine milk and biscuit mix, stir until smooth, and pour over meat mixture. Bake 25 minutes, uncovered, in 425° oven; spread with sour cream and sprinkle with cheese. Return to oven another 5 minutes. Makes 4-6 servings.

Olivia Miller
Memphis, Tennessee
December 21, 1993

Swedish Meatballs

When Ellen came from Sweden as the bride of a handsome American, she brought along this recipe that had been in her family for more than 100 years. She said that just as turkey is a treat to us on holidays, these special meatballs were a treat to her people, whose everyday diet consisted of fish—and more fish.

2 lbs. ground round steak
1 lb. ground pork steak
2 eggs, beaten
1 cup mashed potatoes
1 cup bread crumbs
1 tsp. brown sugar
1½ tsps. salt
½ tsp. black pepper
1 tsp. ginger
½ tsp. nutmeg
½ tsp. cloves
½ tsp. allspice
1 cup milk, OR ½ cup evaporated cream and ½ cup cold water

Mix together all ingredients except milk and form into soft balls. Roll balls in flour. Fry on all sides in a small amount of fat until balls are brown. Pour the milk over meatballs and cook over moderate heat for 30 minutes. Recipe makes 25 meatballs and furnishes a delicious meat course.

Grace Schoonover
Topeka, Kansas
December 27, 1955

Spaghetti and Meatballs, Family Style

These rich, flavorful meatballs boast a hint of cheese.

1   lb. ground beef
¾   cup finely crushed cheese crackers
2   Tbsps. Worcestershire sauce
⅓   cup chopped OR minced onion
1   tsp. salt
½   tsp. hot pepper sauce
½   tsp. pepper
12 ozs. vegetable juice cocktail
•   dash garlic salt
2   8-oz. cans spaghetti sauce with mushrooms
1   lb. spaghetti
•   additional cheese cracker crumbs OR Parmesan cheese

Combine ground beef, cheese cracker crumbs, Worcestershire sauce, onion, salt, hot pepper sauce and pepper. Mix well and form into about 16 balls.

Bring vegetable juice cocktail to boil in heavy skillet. Add garlic salt and meatballs. Reduce heat and simmer, uncovered, about 20 minutes, until liquid is reduced to about ½ cup. Add spaghetti sauce and heat. (Two cups of sauce prepared from a dry mix may be used, if preferred.) Meanwhile, cook spaghetti as directed. Serve meatballs and sauce over spaghetti, sprinkling with additional cheese cracker crumbs or Parmesan cheese. Makes 4-5 servings.

Mrs. P.L. Browns
Denver, Colorado
March 1, 1994

COOKING PASTA

The only way to know when pasta is done is to taste it. The term "al dente" is used to describe pasta that is done correctly. It means "to the tooth," not too hard, not too soft, just right when you bite into it.

When cooking dried pasta, you may want to begin tasting it after 4 minutes of cooking, depending on its shape and size. Remove a noodle, let it cool briefly, and cut it in half. If you no longer see any dry, white, uncooked pasta in the middle, it's done. Remember: fresh pastas should be checked for doneness after only 30 seconds.

Marvelous Meatballs

My family loves these meat-balls. They are moist and so tasty.

2   **cups crushed corn flakes**
3   **Tbsps. diced onion**
1½ **lbs. ground beef**
½   **tsp. salt**
•   **pepper to taste**
1   **egg**
⅔   **cup applesauce**
½   **cup catsup**
1   **cup tomato soup**
½   **cup water**
2½ **cups tomato juice**

Mix corn flakes, diced onion, ground beef, salt, pepper, egg and applesauce. Shape into balls (about 24). Place meat-balls in a 9x13-inch baking pan. Cover with a mixture of catsup, soup, water and toma-to juice. Bake for 1 hour in a 350° oven.

Bobbie Mae Cooley
Bowen, Illinois
November 9, 1993

Beans and Meatballs

This is an easy casserole. Served with a tossed salad and hot rolls, this makes a tempting meal on wintery days.

1   **lb. ground beef**
½   **cup evaporated milk**
⅔   **cup bread crumbs**
1   **tsp. salt**
•   **dash of pepper**
1   **cup sliced onion**
1   **lb. can of baked beans**
2   **Tbsps. catsup**
¼   **tsp. dry mustard**

Combine the first 5 ingredi-ents. With wet hands form into 16 meatballs. Brown in large skillet along with onions. Cover and cook over low heat for 10 minutes. Add beans, catsup and mustard. Cover and heat for 15 minutes. Makes 6 servings.

Shirley M. Ziemke
State Center, Iowa
December 4, 1990

■ Holiday Best ■

Thanksgiving brings out the very best —
The linen cloth from the cedar chest,
Bone china long in the family,
The silver polished carefully;
Best manners for the guests we greet,
The brownest bird, the sweetest treat;
And hearts most grateful, joined in prayer
For home and loved ones gathered there.

— Betty Wallace Scott

Hearty Swirled Meat Loaf with Cheese

2 lbs. lean ground beef
2 cups soft bread crumbs
2 eggs, lightly beaten
½ cup grated Parmesan cheese
2 Tbsps. instant minced onion
1 tsp. Italian seasoning, crushed
1 tsp. salt
¼ tsp. ground black pepper
½ cup milk
1 10-oz. pkg. frozen chopped spinach, thawed and very well drained
1 8-oz. pkg. shredded sharp Cheddar cheese (2 cups)

Preheat oven to 350°. In a large bowl place beef, bread crumbs, eggs, Parmesan cheese, onion, Italian seasoning, salt, black pepper and milk; mix just until combined. Place a 12x12-inch sheet of plastic wrap on a work surface. Place meat mixture on plastic wrap; pat into a 9x12-inch rectangle. Spoon spinach over meat to within ½ inch from all edges; sprinkle spinach with 1½ cups of Cheddar cheese. Starting at a narrow side, roll up jelly-roll style. Place roll seam-side down in an ungreased shallow roasting pan. Bake until juices run clear when a knife is inserted near the center, about 1 hour and 15 minutes; 5 minutes before removing from the oven sprinkle the top with the remaining ½ cup Cheddar cheese. Let stand 5 minutes before serving. Makes 8 servings.

Editor's Note: Leftover meat loaf may be cut into individual portions, then securely wrapped and frozen. To defrost and reheat in the microwave: unwrap, place on a microwaveable plate, cover lightly and heat only until hot.

Kate Marchbanks Food Story
May 10, 1994

Super Meat Loaf

This meat loaf is good enough for a company dinner.

Filling:
- 1 cup fresh OR canned sliced mushrooms, drained
- ½ cup chopped onion
- 2 Tbsps. butter OR margarine
- ⅓ cup sour cream

Meat Loaf:
- 1½ lbs. ground beef
- ¼ cup quick oats, uncooked
- 1 egg
- ¼ tsp. pepper
- 1½ tsps. salt
- 1 tsp. Worcestershire sauce
- ⅔ cup milk

For filling, lightly brown mushrooms and onion in butter or margarine in medium-size skillet. Remove from heat; stir in sour cream.

For meat loaf, thoroughly combine ground beef, oats, egg, pepper, salt, Worcestershire sauce and milk. Place half of meat mixture in shallow baking pan. Shape to form an oval base. Lengthwise down the center make a shallow "well" for filling, making sure all filling is covered by other half of meat mixture. Seal together bottom and top of meat mixture. Bake at 350° for 1 hour. Let stand 10 minutes before slicing. Makes 6 servings.

Louise Mayer
Richmond, Virginia
February 1, 1994

Horseradish Beef Pot Roast

This is very tender and good.

- 1 3- to 4-lb. boneless beef bottom round
- 2 Tbsps. oil
- 1 tsp. salt
- ⅛ tsp. pepper
- ¼ cup tomato juice
- ¼ cup prepared horseradish
- ½ cup chopped onion
- ¼ cup water
- 2 Tbsps. flour

Brown pot roast in oil in large frying pan. Pour off drippings. Season pot roast with salt and pepper. Add tomato juice, horseradish and onion. Cover tightly and cook slowly 2½-3½ hours or until meat is tender. Remove pot roast to warm platter. Combine flour with ¼ cup water, add to cooking liquid and cook, stirring constantly until thickened. Reduce heat and cook 3-5 minutes. Serve gravy with pot roast

Mrs. Harriet Bien
Rome, New York
April 24, 1990

Pepsi Pork Roast

We like the flavor. The pop doesn't make it too sweet. You may want to place a few potatoes around the roast, because there will be plenty of good gravy.

1   4- to 6-lb. pork roast
½   pkg. dry onion soup mix
1   can cream of mushroom soup
1   can Pepsi Cola

Place roast in pan or Crock-Pot. Add dry onion soup mix, cream of mushroom soup and cola. Bake in oven between 250-300° for 3-4 hours. Consult your instruction book for Crock-Pot method. Any leftovers make good pork sandwiches later.

Aletha J. Hansen
Kimballton, Iowa
December 22, 1987

Lasagne

This recipe requires no pre-cooking of the noodles.

1   lb. hamburger
1   32-oz. spaghetti sauce
9   strips lasagne noodles, uncooked
1   15-oz. container drained cottage cheese or ricotta cheese
12   ozs. grated mozzarella cheese

Brown hamburger and drain. Add spaghetti sauce. In a greased 9x13-inch pan, place a small amount of meat sauce. Layer uncooked lasagne noodles, meat sauce, cottage cheese and mozzarella cheese in 3 layers. Bake covered in 375° oven for 30 minutes. Remove cover and bake an additional 30 minutes. Let stand 10 minutes before cutting.

JoAnn Lees
Avoca, Iowa
July 19, 1988

Crafty Crescent Lasagne

This is one of our favorites.

Meat Filling:
- 1 lb. hamburger
- ¾ cup chopped onion
- 1 Tbsp. parsley flakes
- ½ tsp. basil
- ½ tsp. oregano
- 1 6-oz. can tomato paste
- ½ tsp. salt, if desired

Cheese Filling:
- 1 cup creamed small curd cottage cheese
- 1 egg
- ¼ cup grated Parmesan cheese

Crust:
- 2 cans crescent dinner rolls
- 2 4x7-inch slices mozzarella cheese
- 1 Tbsp. milk
- 1 Tbsp. sesame seeds

To make meat filling: Brown meat, drain well, add seasoning and tomato paste. Simmer uncovered 5 minutes. (This can be made ahead and placed in the refrigerator.)

To make cheese filling: Combine cottage cheese, egg and Parmesan cheese.

To make crust: Unroll crescent dinner rolls; separate into 8 rectangles. Place side by side on ungreased cookie sheet, overlapping edges slightly to form 13x15-inch rectangle. Spread half of meat filling lengthwise down center of dough within 1 inch of each end. Top meat filling with cheese filling. Spoon remaining meat filling over top, forming 3 layers. Place cheese slices over meat filling; fold 13-inch ends over filling 1 inch. Pull long sides of dough rectangle over filling, being careful to overlap edges only ¼ inch. Pinch overlapped edges. Brush with milk; sprinkle with sesame seeds. Bake in 375° oven for 30 minutes or until golden brown.

Barbara S. Davis
Pratt, Kansas
August 13, 1991

■ Bon Appetit! ■

I guess my turkey-cooking's
Up to snuff
My turkey-eaters never
Cry, "Enough!"
It's more than just the turkey
That I stuff!

— **Maureen Cannon**

Zucchini Beef Casserole

I'd like to share this good recipe.

1 lb. ground beef
⅓ cup onion, chopped
1 clove garlic, minced
1 can (2 cups) tomatoes
¾ cup rice
2 Tbsps. Worcestershire sauce
• salt and pepper to taste
1 cup shredded Cheddar cheese
2 large zucchini, sliced but unpeeled
½ cup shredded Monterey Jack cheese
1 cup sour cream
½ cup shredded Cheddar cheese

Brown ground beef, onion and garlic. Add tomatoes, rice, Worcestershire sauce, salt and pepper. Cook until rice is tender. Add 1 cup Cheddar cheese. Cook zucchini in small amount of water until tender, about 7 minutes.

In a 2-quart baking dish, layer half of meat mixture, then well-drained zucchini, Monterey Jack cheese, remaining half of meat mixture, sour cream and top with ½ cup Cheddar cheese. Bake in 350° oven 25-30 minutes.

Marjorie Hottman
Abilene, Kansas
September 1, 1981

Poor Man's Steak

This is one of my favorites.

3 lbs. hamburger
1 cup milk
1 cup bread OR cracker crumbs
¼ cup grated onion, optional
1 can mushroom soup OR celery soup
1 can water

Mix together meat, milk, crumbs and onion. Spread on cookie sheet or put in 9x12-inch pan if you want thicker pieces. Cover and place in refrigerator for at least 3 hours or overnight. Cut into squares; flour and brown in skillet before placing in large baking pan. Cover with soup and water. Bake in 350° oven for 1 hour.

Dorothy Holifield
Irondale, Missouri
October 10, 1989

Restaurant Chili

This is the original chili recipe from a well-known restaurant. I would like others to enjoy this wonderful chili as we have for many years.

½ lb. pinto beans
5 cups canned tomatoes
1 lb. chopped green peppers
1½ Tbsps. salad oil
1½ lbs. chopped onions
2 cloves crushed garlic
½ cup chopped parsley
½ cup butter
2½ lbs. ground beef chuck
1 lb. ground lean pork
⅓ cup chili powder
2 Tbsps. salt
1½ tsps. pepper
1½ tsps. cumin seed
1½ tsps. monosodium glutamate

Wash beans, soak overnight in water 2 inches above beans. Simmer, covered, in same water until tender. Add tomatoes and simmer 5 minutes. Sauté green pepper in salad oil 5 minutes. Add onion, cook until tender, stirring often.

Add garlic and parsley. Melt butter and sauté meat for 15 minutes. Add meat to onion mixture, stir in chili powder and cook 10 minutes. Add this to beans; add spices. Simmer, covered, for 1 hour. Cook uncovered 30 minutes. Skim fat from top. Makes 4 quarts and freezes well.

Doris L. Dill
Lone Pine, California
November 20, 1990

TREAT ASSURES GOOD LUCK
In Denmark, Sweden and Norway, it is said that a magical little "Nisse" lives in every household.
During the holidays, children put out a treat of homemade porridge for the mischievous creature to ward off bad luck in the coming year.

■ EASY MEAT GLAZES
Use your favorite preserves, jams and jellies as glazes on beef, pork and poultry:
Pork: Pineapple, apricot, cherry, peach or sweet orange marmalade.
Poultry: Cherry, red raspberry, peach, apricot or pineapple preserves.
Beef: Currant or quince jelly.

Crock Pizza

Serve with a salad for a complete meal.

1　12-oz. pkg. kluski noodles
1½　lbs. ground beef
1　medium onion, chopped
1　16-oz. jar pizza sauce
1　8-oz. jar spaghetti sauce
•　mushroom and green pepper, optional
8　ozs. Cheddar cheese, shredded
8　ozs. mozzarella cheese, shredded
1　pkg. pepperoni, sliced

Cook and drain noodles. Brown ground beef and onions. Drain off fat. Add the sauces and optional ingredients to the meat and simmer well. Layer, twice; noodles, meat sauce, Cheddar cheese, mozzarella cheese and pepperoni.

Turn Crock-Pot on low and serve when the cheese is melted, or set on high for approximately 30 minutes.

Or layer in a 9x13-inch baking pan and bake in 350° oven for 20 minutes or until cheese is melted. Makes 12 servings.

Magdalena Stutzman
Sullivan, Illinois
September 13, 1989

Easy Microwave Pizza Breads

These are always a hit.

1½　lbs. ground beef
1　qt. spaghetti sauce
1　loaf French bread
1　large onion, minced
1　green pepper, minced
8　ozs. fresh mushrooms, sliced
1½　cups cooked bacon, crumbled
1　lb. pepperoni, sliced
½　cup sliced olives
16　ozs. mozzarella cheese

Brown ground meat, add spaghetti sauce and cook until hot. Cut loaf of French bread lengthwise and top each half with meat sauce. Add onions, peppers, mushrooms, bacon, pepperoni, olives and whatever else you like on pizza; top with mozzarella cheese. Cut each half in 4 sections. Cook in microwave until cheese melts.

Stacy Pickett
Ozawkie, Kansas
November 6, 1990

Cranberry and Bean Casserole

1   lb. hamburger
1   large onion
1   large (20¾ oz.) can pork and beans
1   15-oz. can cranberries
¼   cup catsup
½   cup brown sugar OR to taste
•   salt
•   pepper

Brown hamburger and onion together. Drain. Add beans, cranberries, catsup, brown sugar and seasonings. Pour into 9x13-inch pan. Heat in 350-375° oven until bubbly on top.

Vicki Schlereth Peterson
Dodge City, Kansas
June 24, 1986

Sweet Barbecue Pork Chops

These chops are delicious.

½   cup onions, chopped
½   cup brown sugar
½   cup catsup
6   Tbsps. vinegar
2   tsps. Worcestershire sauce
•   salt to taste
•   pepper to taste
10   pork chops

Combine all ingredients, except pork chops, in saucepan and bring to a boil. Simmer for 5 minutes. Makes enough sauce for 10 pork chops. Spoon sauce over chops and bake in 375° oven for 1 hour and 45 minutes.

Gladys M. Hanes
Fort Scott, Kansas
October 24, 1989

70

Sausage Apple Bean Bake

One of my favorite recipes!

2   1-lb. cans pork and beans
4   cups cooked apple slices
¼   cup brown sugar
1   Tbsp. prepared mustard
½   Tbsp. lemon juice
1   tsp. Worcestershire sauce
2   lbs. sausage links

Combine beans and apples. Combine brown sugar, mustard, lemon juice and Worcestershire sauce; stir into bean-apple mixture. Cut sausage links into bite-size pieces, brown in skillet and drain. Add to bean-apple mixture, pour into casserole pan and bake at 350° until bubbly.

Lucile Metcalf
Squaw Valley, California
April 26, 1994

Cheese and Sausage Bake

This dish is easy to make, and keeps kitchen clean-up to a minimum.

1   lb. bulk sausage
3½ cups biscuit mix
1   10-oz. pkg. shredded cheese

Combine all ingredients. Spread over large baking dish and bake at 350° for 20-30 minutes, or until sausage is done.

Brenda East
Victor, Montana
January 18, 1994

Manicotti

This is delicious served with garlic bread.

1   pkg. mild Italian
    sausage
1   12-oz. can tomato
    sauce OR Italian
    tomato sauce
1   small can tomato
    paste
1   small can water
•   salt and pepper to
    taste
½   tsp. garlic powder
½   tsp. oregano
1   small box of fresh,
    sliced mushrooms
1   box manicotti
    shells

Filling:
1   container ricotta
    cheese
3   cups mozzarella,
    shredded
1   cup Parmesan
    cheese
1   pkg. frozen
    chopped spinach
    OR 8 ozs. fresh
    spinach, chopped
    fine
1   egg
•   salt and pepper to
    taste

Squeeze sausage out of casing into a hot kettle. (I do this portion in my Crock-Pot, all day on low.) Brown. Add tomato sauce, tomato paste and water. Add salt, pepper, garlic powder and oregano.

Add the sliced mushrooms 30 minutes before preparing dish.

Boil manicotti shells as directed on box (8-10 minutes), adding some oil to prevent sticking. Drain.

To make the filling, mix 2 cups mozzarella cheese, ricotta and Parmesan. Add spinach, egg, salt and pepper. Stuff manicotti with cheese mixture, using a small spoon.

Put some of the sausage sauce on the bottom of a 9x13-inch pan. Place stuffed manicotti in rows so they are not touching. Pour remaining sauce on top. Sprinkle with remaining 1 cup of mozzarella. Bake in 350° oven until cheese bubbles.

Pat L. Williams
Aledo, Illinois
November 7, 1989

■ Snakes on the Counter Top ■

*Every time my grandma worked
With her keen-edged noodle cutter,
I recall how serpents lurked
In the doughy, tangled clutter.*

— **Richard Franklin**

Scrapple

This is good for breakfast or just about anytime!

1 lb. bulk pork sausage
3 chicken bouillon cubes
3½ cups boiling water
1 cup yellow corn meal
¼ tsp. salt
⅛ tsp. dried thyme, crushed

In electric skillet, set at 350°, brown sausage slowly, stirring to break into small pieces; drain off fat. Dissolve bouillon cubes in boiling water, add to sausage. Bring to boiling. Slowly stir in corn meal, salt and thyme. Cook 10 minutes stirring constantly. Pour into greased 4x8x2-inch loaf pan. Chill until firm or overnight.

To serve, unmold the mixture and cut into ½-inch thick slices. Dip in corn meal and slowly brown the coated slices, about 8 minutes on each side. Serve with butter and syrup, if desired. Makes 6 servings.

Mrs. C. Sisson
Luray, Missouri
February 12, 1985

Good Morning Casserole

I come from a family of 10 kids and every last one of us loves this casserole.

2 12-oz. pkgs. link sausages
8 slices bread
2 cups grated Cheddar cheese
4 eggs
2½ cups milk
1 can cream of mushroom soup

Brown sausages and cut into ¼-inch pieces. Cube bread and place in 9x13x2-inch pan. Spread sausage pieces and cheese over bread. Add milk to beaten eggs and pour over bread mixture. Spread undiluted cream of mushroom soup over the top. Bake in 325° oven for 1 hour.

Elizabeth Keim
Bronson, Michigan
May 28, 1992

Cheese and Potato Wild Rice Soup

This is really good soup.

½ cup wild rice, uncooked
1½ cups water
½ lb. bacon, cut in pieces
¼ cup chopped onion
2 10¾-oz. cans cream of potato soup
1 soup can filled with ½ water and ½ milk
1 qt. milk
2½ cups grated American cheese
• grated or curled carrots, optional

Combine wild rice and water in kettle. Cook over low heat for 45 minutes. Drain. Set aside.

Fry bacon and onion in skillet until bacon is crisp. Drain bacon and onion on paper towel. Place soup in large pan; dilute with 1 can half milk and half water. Stir in quart of milk, bacon, onion, cheese and cooked rice. Stir until cheese is melted. Add carrot curls or grated carrot to garnish. Makes 8-10 servings.

Mary Kay Winter
Shell Rock, Iowa
October 9, 1990

Monterey Pizza Rice

1 10¾-oz. can condensed chicken broth
1 cup rice
1 cup water
¾ cup pizza sauce
1 3-4 oz. pkg. sliced pepperoni
1 4-oz. can mushroom stems and pieces, drained
½ cup chopped onion
1 tsp. fennel seeds
½ cup chopped green pepper
½ cup (2 ozs.) shredded Monterey Jack cheese

Combine all ingredients except green pepper and cheese in 10-inch skillet. Bring to a boil; reduce heat. Cover and simmer 20 minutes. Stir in green pepper; remove from heat. Let stand covered 5 minutes or until all liquid is absorbed. Sprinkle with cheese. Makes 5 servings.

Kate Marchbanks Food Story
April 9, 1991

Best-Ever Turkey Casserole

Melted cheese and mushroom soup give this casserole a rich flavor.

1 box wild long-grain rice mix, prepared according to directions
4-6 cups turkey, cooked and chopped
2 boxes frozen broccoli, cooked
1 cup mushrooms
1 8-oz. can water chestnuts, sliced
8 ozs. sliced cheese
1 can chicken broth
1 can cream of mushroom soup
½ cup Miracle Whip
1 can french-fried onion rings

Layer rice mix, turkey, broccoli, mushrooms, water chestnuts and cheese in a 9x13-inch casserole dish. Pour chicken broth over top. Cover with mixture of cream of mushroom soup and Miracle Whip.
Bake 45 minutes at 350°. Spread onion rings on top for final 5-10 minutes of baking.

Bernice Knutson
Soldier, Iowa
May 24, 1994

Yum-Yum Casserole

This is delicious!

1 6-oz. box long grain OR wild rice, cooked
1 lb. broccoli, steamed
3 cups cooked chicken OR ham
2 cups shredded cheese, Cheddar OR mozzarella
2 cups fresh OR canned mushrooms
1 cup mayonnaise
1 can cream of celery soup
¼ tsp. dry mustard
¼ tsp. curry powder
1 cup crushed croutons
2 Tbsps. margarine
¼ cup grated Parmesan cheese

Spray coat a 9x13-inch pan. Layer rice, broccoli, meat, cheese and mushrooms into pan. Combine soup, mayonnaise, mustard and curry. Pour over layers. Combine crushed croutons and margarine. Top the layers. Sprinkle with Parmesan cheese. Bake in 350° oven for 30 minutes.

Pat Williams
Aledo, Illinois
March 13, 1990

Baked Chicken Puff

Leftover chicken or turkey will go well in this recipe.

1   can condensed cream of mush-room soup
⅓   cup milk
½   tsp. salt
1   cup diced, cooked turkey OR chicken
2   cups cooked peas, green beans OR broccoli
4   eggs, separated
⅓   cup grated Cheddar cheese

Combine undiluted soup, milk and salt in a 1½-quart casserole. Add chicken and peas. Bake 10 minutes in a preheated 375° oven. Beat egg whites until stiff, then beat egg yolks with the same beater. Add cheese and carefully fold yolks into the whites. Pile on top of the chicken mixture. Bake another 30 minutes. Makes 6 servings.

Doris Williams
Brainerd, Minnesota
January 17, 1989

Chicken Breasts with Asparagus

A colorful and delicious dish to serve.

1   Tbsp. cooking oil
4   chicken breasts, skinned, boned and halved
1   can cream of asparagus soup
⅓   cup milk
½   tsp. white pepper
¾   lb. fresh asparagus spears, cut up OR 1 10-oz. pkg. frozen asparagus cuts

In skillet, over medium-high heat in hot oil, cook chicken 10 minutes or until browned. Remove and set aside. Spoon off fat. In skillet, combine soup, milk and white pepper. Stir in asparagus. Heat to boiling. Return chicken to skillet. Cover; cook over low heat for 10 minutes or until chicken is no longer pink and asparagus is tender-crisp, stirring often. Makes 4 servings.

Mildred Sherrer
Bay City, Texas
April 26, 1994

Oven Barbecued Chicken

Everyone wants this recipe.

5-6 lbs. chicken thighs
•   garlic powder
3   eggs, beaten
2   cups granulated
     sugar
1   cup pineapple juice
1½   cups catsup
1   cup white vinegar
2   tsps. soy sauce

Wash chicken thighs and pat dry. Sprinkle with garlic powder and let set for about 5 minutes. Dip chicken in beaten eggs. Fry until nearly done. Spray large oven pan with non-stick spray. Mix together the granulated sugar, juice, catsup, vinegar and soy sauce. Put chicken in pan and pour the sauce over chicken. Cover pan with aluminum foil and bake 30-45 minutes in 300° oven, or until sauce is thick. Put chicken on platter and spoon remaining sauce over top.

Helen Peter
St. Francis, Kansas
May 21, 1991

Baked Chicken Breasts with Cranberry Sauce

Here's a favorite chicken recipe.

6   chicken breasts,
     skin removed
1   can whole cranberry
     sauce
½   cup Catalina
     dressing
½   pkg. dry onion
     soup mix

Place chicken breasts in greased 9x13-inch pan. Heat together can of cranberry sauce, Catalina dressing and dry onion soup mix. Pour over chicken breasts, cover. Bake at 350° for 50-60 minutes.

Bertha Helmers
Titonka, Iowa
July 5, 1994

■ Second Thoughts ■

*It's not the minutes of a meal
that add the extra pound
but rather it's the seconds
that tend to make us round.*

— Juliana Lewis

Chicken Dressing Casserole

1   3-lb. fryer chicken
1   can cream of mushroom soup
1   can cream of chicken soup
1   13-oz. can evaporated milk
1   8-oz. pkg. top-of-stove stuffing mix
½   cup melted butter
½   cup chicken broth

Cook chicken and remove bones. (Reserve ½ cup broth.) Cut chicken into bite-size pieces. Combine soups, milk and broth. Heat thoroughly. Combine stuffing mix and melted butter. Spread half of stuffing in a greased 9x13-inch pan. Layer chicken over this then pour soups over and top with remaining stuffing. Bake uncovered for 35 minutes at 350°.

Mabel Hossel
Olney, Illinois
February 27, 1990

Chicken Breasts, Picnic Style

This is quick to put together and may be prepared the night before, then baked the next day. This sauce is so good.

8   chicken breasts, skinned and boned
8   strips of bacon
2   small (2½-oz. size) jars dried beef
1   10¾-oz. can chicken soup
1   cup sour cream

Preheat oven to 275°. Wrap each chicken breast with a strip of bacon and secure with toothpick. Place chipped beef in bottom of glass 9x13-inch baking dish. Top with chicken. Mix soup and sour cream together and pour over chicken. Bake, uncovered, 3 hours. The secret is the low baking temperature.

Virginia Fitch
Enid, Oklahoma
July 16, 1991

SEASONED BUTTER
Seasoned (compound) butter makes an "instant sauce" to serve over grilled meat, poultry, seafood or vegetables. To make seasoned butter:

■ Combine softened butter with seasonings such as chili powder, garlic powder and basil, curry powder, lemon and tarragon or spicy mustard.

■ Shape into a log on plastic wrap or foil and wrap tightly. Refrigerate or freeze.

■ When food is ready to serve, top it with a thin slice of the seasoned butter or melt and drizzle butter over the food.

Quick Low-Fat Raspberry Chicken

This chicken is good served over rice with steamed vegetables.

4   chicken breasts, skinned, boned and halved
5   ozs. raspberry fruit-sweetened preserves
½   cup pineapple juice
¼   cup low-sodium soy sauce
2   Tbsps. cider vinegar
½   tsp. chili powder
½   tsp. garlic powder
½   cup fresh OR frozen (thawed) raspberries

Place chicken breasts in baking dish. Combine preserves, pineapple juice, soy sauce, vinegar, chili powder and garlic powder and blend well. Pour sauce over breasts. Cover and marinate in refrigerator for a few hours. Preheat oven to 350°. Bake chicken in its sauce for 30 minutes or microwave for 15-20 minutes.

Serve ½ breast per person, garnished with fresh or thawed frozen raspberries.

Liz Fernald
Mashpee, Massachusetts
July 19, 1994

Chicken Pot Pie

This is one of my favorites.

2   10¾-oz. cans cream of potato soup
1   16-oz. can mixed vegetables, drained
2   cups cooked, diced chicken
½   cup milk
½   tsp. thyme
½   tsp. black pepper
2   9-inch pie crusts, thawed
1   egg slightly beaten, optional

Combine first 6 ingredients. Spoon into prepared pie crust. Cover with top crust, crimp edges to seal. Slit top crust and brush with egg, if desired. Bake in 375° oven for 40 minutes.

Cara Bauer
Longmont, Colorado
April 9, 1991

Kathie's Artichoke Bake

Here's a yummy recipe for any meal. I've served this at a holiday buffet but especially enjoy it for brunch with my favorite muffin recipe and frozen fruit slush.

Casserole:
- 4 Tbsps. butter
- 4 Tbsps. flour
- 2 cups skim milk
- ⅛ tsp. black pepper
- 1 8-oz. carton fat-free cream cheese
- 1 large bunch fresh broccoli
- ½ medium-sized onion, chopped
- 2 14-oz. cans artichoke hearts packed in water, drained
- 1 8-oz. pkg. chunk style imitation king crab meat
- 4 ozs. fat-free shredded Cheddar cheese

Topping:
- 2 cups soft bread crumbs
- 2 Tbsps. butter, melted

For casserole, melt butter; add flour and milk to make a white sauce. Season with pepper. Remove from heat and stir in cream cheese. Cut up broccoli and cook with onion in microwave until tender. Place broccoli, onion, artichoke hearts and crab meat in bottom of greased 9x13-inch pan. Pour cream cheese white sauce over artichoke mixture. Sprinkle Cheddar cheese over sauce. For topping, toss bread crumbs with butter; sprinkle over cheese. Bake at 350° for 30 minutes.

Kathie Netley
Omaha, Nebraska
December 6, 1994

80

Tuna Rolls

I thought I'd lost this recipe, so I was thrilled when it reappeared. I think you'll like it too.

- 1   9¼-oz. can light tuna in water, well drained
- 1   cup (4 ozs.) shredded Cheddar cheese
- ¼   cup coarsely chopped ripe olives
- ¼   cup coarsely chopped pecans
- ¼   cup chopped red OR green pepper
- ¼   cup chopped green onions and tops
- 1   Tbsp. dill weed
- 1   16-oz. pkg. hot roll mix
- 1   cup hot water
- 2   Tbsps. vegetable oil
- 1   egg

Combine tuna, cheese, pecans, olives, pepper, onions and dill weed. Make hot roll mix according to package directions. Knead dough on floured surface until smooth and elastic, 3-5 minutes. Let stand 5 minutes. Roll dough on floured surface into rectangle 12x16-inches; sprinkle tuna mixture over dough, leaving 1-inch border on all sides. Roll up, beginning with long sides. Pinch seams to seal. To make rolls, trim ends of dough roll; gently stretch dough roll until 18 inches long. Cut into 18 individual rolls; place cut-side down ¾ inch apart on greased baking sheet. Bake in 375° oven until golden, about 20-25 minutes. Cool on wire racks. Serve warm. Makes 18 rolls.

Mrs. Bruce S. Henderson
Mesa, Arizona
March 28, 1989

DINNER TIPS FOR WORKING PARENTS

Advance meal planning, simple food, keeping the freezer and pantry shelves stocked with basics and double- and triple-batch cooking are all big time-savers for working moms and dads.

It's just as easy to cook 2 chickens as 1, and the second can show up in a different dish at the second meal.

In the summertime, one can grill boneless chicken breasts and several different meats at 1 time and then freeze them to use in salads and sandwiches later. In cool weather, make 2 pans of vegetable lasagne or a huge batch of chili. Both reheat beautifully in the microwave. A double batch of vegetables roasted for 1 meal can appear at the second meal teamed with cheeses like mozzarella and Parmesan and used as a topping for focaccia (Italian flat bread) or Italian bread shells.

Another favorite meal is breakfast for supper—a hit with the kids. Try French toast, cheese and vegetable omelets or traditional pancakes and sausage.

Seafood Enchiladas

I made this for one family get together and it was a big hit.

2 10-oz. cans 99 percent fat-free cream of chicken soup
1 10-oz. pkg. frozen, chopped spinach, thawed and drained
½ cup chopped onion
1 8-oz. pkg. chopped mock crab
1¾ cups reduced fat Monterey Jack cheese, shredded
• dash ground nutmeg
8 6-inch flour OR corn tortillas

Mix 1 can of soup, spinach, onion, mock crab, 1 cup of cheese and dash of nutmeg. Place half of second can of soup on the bottom of a 7x11-inch microwave-safe baking dish. Divide the crab mixture evenly among the tortillas. Roll and place in the baking dish, seam-side down. Pour remaining soup over the top of tortillas. Sprinkle with nutmeg. Cook, covered, on high in microwave for 7 minutes. Turn. Cook another 5 minutes on medium high. Sprinkle remaining cheese on top. Let stand 5 minutes before serving. Makes about 4 servings.

Kathie Netley
Omaha, Nebraska
March 29, 1994

Tuna Burgers

Serve warm from oven.

1 cup cubed American cheese
3 hard-cooked eggs
1 7-oz. can tuna
2 Tbsps. chopped green pepper
2 Tbsps. chopped onion
2 Tbsps. chopped olives, optional
2 Tbsps. chopped sweet pickle
½ cup mayonnaise
• hot dog buns

Toss ingredients, except buns, together lightly. Split buns and butter generously; spread with filling. Wrap each filled bun individually in foil. Bake in 350° oven for 20-30 minutes.

Mrs. Mervin Van Tiger
Kennewick, Washington
September 26, 1957

Veggie Pizza

Hope you enjoy this as we do. I made it for Anna's baptism.

- **2 tubes refrigerated crescent rolls**
- **2 8-oz. pkgs. cream cheese, softened**
- **⅔ cup mayonnaise**
- **¼ tsp. dill weed**
- **½ tsp. minced onion**
- **raw vegetables: carrots, cauliflower, celery, broccoli, cucumbers, tomatoes, lettuce and olives**
- **grated cheese**

Spread crescent rolls on cookie sheet, pinching seams together. Bake in 350-375° oven for 10 minutes. Cool. Whip cream cheese, mayonnaise, dill weed and minced onion. Spread mixture on cooled crust. Top with raw veggies, then grated cheese.

Aletha J. Hansen
Kimballton, Iowa
August 29, 1989

KEEPING SPICES POTENT

A selection of dried herbs and spices are essential to every cook's pantry. Spices are almost always purchased in dried form, since most often it is the aromatic and flavoring agents such as seeds or bark that give food pungency. Dried herbs and spices are more powerful than fresh ones, so it is wise to use them with some restraint, especially if the dish is to simmer and reduce in volume during cooking, such as soups or stews.

■ Heat, light and time are the enemies of spices, so perhaps the worst place to store them is in a rack over the stove in glass jars. Place a small piece of masking tape on the lid, and mark the date it was purchased. A general rule is to never keep dried herbs and spices for more than 1 year. If the spice is one that is only used occasionally, buy the smallest size jar, or keep infrequently-used jars in the basement where it may be cooler. Store the jars or tins inside your coolest closet or cabinet.

■ The best tests for freshness are color and aroma. If the spice smells potent and the color is the same as it was the day it was purchased, it is probably still good.

■ If you stock many spice jars in a closet, the best way to save time is to shelve them in alphabetical order.

■ Bacon Gravy ■

The recipes of bygone days
Are written much about,
But as to olden gravies
They are just about left out.

This old-time gravy once was called
By milk or flour or bacon,
But it was all the very same
When it was in the makin'!

The bacon would be fried till brown
Then taken from the pan,
Some flour stirred into the grease
And browned till it was tan.

Then milk poured in and seasonings
And stirred till thick and nice—
A call that it was time to eat
Need never be made twice.

This truly was a special time
For Sally, Sue and Davey—
When soaking homemade biscuits in
Their plates of bacon gravy.

— Rachel Hartnett

■ Tasting the World ■

Spicy air, a street
soaked in aroma,
cooks mixing
their flavors
in a democracy
of air space,
without the loss
of sovereignty.
I travel sans passport.

— Carol Hamilton

84

On The Side

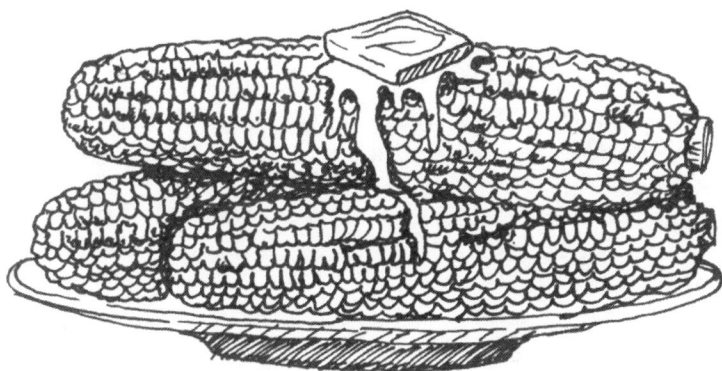

■ On The Side ■

Broccoli Soup 87
Noodle Soup and Butter Balls 88
Potato Supreme 88
Summer Squash Surprise 89
Swedish Bean Bake 89
Baked Cabbage Casserole 90
Onion Pie 90
Vegetable Pudding 91
Tuna Cauliflower Fiesta 91
Reunion Scalloped Potatoes 92
Swiss Green Bean Casserole 92
Chiffon Sweet Potato Pie 93
Broccoli Puff 94
Danish Limas 94
Curried Bean and Rice Salad 95
Corn Bread Salad 95
Thai Chicken and Vegetable Salad .96
Fruited Chicken Salad 97
Shoestring Salad 97
You Won't Believe It Isn't Potato Salad 98
Beet Salad 98
Broccoli Salad 99
Greengage Plum Salad 99
Polynesian Coleslaw 100
Broccoli-Cauliflower Salad 100
Carrot-Chive Salad 101
Artichoke Salad 101
Spinach-Orange Salad 102
Asparagus Salad 102
Rice Fruit Salad 103
Sweet-Sour Cabbage 103
Summer Green Bean Salad 104
Tomato Aspic Extraordinaire 104

Broccoli Soup

I've won several prizes with this recipe in contests and cook-offs. It is delicious served with caraway-cheese bread.

1   10-oz. pkg. frozen broccoli OR 12 ozs. fresh broccoli
1   16-oz. can chicken broth
4   Tbsps. margarine
½   medium onion, chopped
1   bay leaf
½   tsp. salt
¼   tsp. pepper
¼   tsp. onion salt
¼   tsp. garlic salt
•   pinch of basil
•   pinch of sage
•   pinch of thyme
•   dash of hot sauce
1   cup milk
¼   cup cream
½   cup buttermilk (1½ Tbsps. dry buttermilk with ½ cup water may be used)
4   Tbsps. flour
2   Tbsps. sour cream
3   Tbsps. margarine

Bring broth to a boil in large kettle. Add broccoli. Simmer until tender. Sauté onion in 2 tablespoons margarine until golden. Add onion to broccoli. Add bay leaf, salt, pepper, onion salt, garlic salt, basil, sage, thyme and hot sauce to mixture. Simmer until all vegetables are tender.

Warm milk, cream and buttermilk. Melt 2 tablespoons margarine in skillet or saucepan. Add flour. Stir. Add warm milk mixture and cook, stirring until thick.

Remove bay leaf from broccoli mixture. Gradually add thickened milk mixture to broccoli. Turn off heat and add 3 tablespoons margarine and sour cream. This is delicious hot or cold. (Cauliflower may be substituted for broccoli.)

Waydella Hart
Bartlett, Kansas
March 17, 1987

Noodle Soup and Butter Balls

Noodle-lovers will go for this combination.

- noodles
- chicken broth
- 4 cups dry fine bread crumbs (1 loaf of bread)
- ¼ lb. butter
- ½ cup cream OR half-and-half
- 4 eggs, slightly beaten
- pinch of allspice, if desired

Cook noodles (as many as you like) in broth until done. Combine crumbs, butter, cream (or half-and-half), eggs and allspice. Shape into balls the size of a walnut. Add to cooking noodles for about 10 minutes. Balls will float.

Ruby Hergenreder
Keenesburg, Colorado
June 6, 1989

Potato Supreme

A tasty potato casserole!

Sauce:
- 4 Tbsps. butter
- 4 Tbsps. flour
- 2 cups milk

Potatoes:
- 2 lbs. grated potatoes
- ½ cup melted butter
- 1 tsp. salt
- ¼ tsp. pepper
- ½ cup chopped onion
- 1 8-oz. pkg. cream cheese

Topping:
- 2 cups crushed corn flakes
- ¼ cup melted butter

To make sauce, melt 4 tablespoons butter and then add flour. Stir until mixed, then add milk, stirring constantly until thickened. If it gets lumpy, beat well until smooth. Mix potatoes, ½ cup melted butter, salt, pepper, onion, cream cheese and sauce together well and place in casserole. Mix corn flakes with ¼ cup melted butter and sprinkle on top of potatoes. Bake at 350° for 1½ hours.

Marilyn Zimmerman
Arbela, Missouri
March 1, 1994

Summer Squash Surprise

This is different, but good.

2   lbs. small summer squash
½   onion
1   carrot
1   cup sour cream
1   10-oz. can cream of chicken soup, undiluted
½   cup melted margarine
1½   cups stuffing mix

Slice the washed squash and onion in the food processor. Cook in 2 tablespoons water for 5 minutes; drain. Grate carrot and mix with sour cream and chicken soup. Add cooked squash and onion. Combine stuffing and melted margarine. In a 2-quart or 8x12-inch baking pan spread half of the stuffing and top with squash mixture. Spread remaining stuffing over squash. Bake at 350° for 25-30 minutes. Makes 6-8 servings.

Helen Daley
Parker, Colorado
September 27, 1994

Swedish Bean Bake

This is a good casserole dish.

1   16-oz. can baked beans
½   large apple, chopped
2   Tbsps. molasses OR 2 Tbsps. raisins
¼   cup onion, chopped
2   Tbsps. brown sugar
½   tsp. dry mustard
2   Tbsps. catsup

Mix all ingredients in a casserole dish. Cover and bake at 300° for about 1 hour. Makes 4-6 servings.

Mildred Tracy
Coyle, Oklahoma
June 20, 1989

Baked Cabbage Casserole

This is so good, even cabbage haters love it.

6 slices white bread
2 cups milk
3 eggs, slightly beaten
• salt to taste
• dash of red pepper
1 onion, grated
2 cups shredded cabbage
½ cup grated cheese

Soak bread in the milk for 5 minutes. Add slightly beaten eggs, salt, pepper, onion and cabbage, mixing well. Top with grated cheese. Bake in 350° oven for 30 minutes.

Mary Smith
Topeka, Kansas
September 12, 1989

Onion Pie

30 small crackers, crushed
½ cup butter
3 cups onions, sliced
¼ cup butter
½ lb. Cheddar cheese, grated
1½ cups milk, scalded
3 eggs, beaten
1 tsp. salt
½ tsp. pepper

Mix the cracker crumbs in ½ cup butter and press into a greased, shallow 2-quart baking dish. Sauté sliced onions in ¼ cup butter, then pour over the cracker crumbs. Sprinkle the grated cheese over the onions. Mix the milk, eggs, salt and pepper. Pour over the cheese. Bake at 350° for 30 minutes or until it is set like a custard.

Magdalena Stutzman
Sullivan, Illinois
April 24, 1990

■ I Draw the Line ■

Health foods today are the pits—
Plus the stems and the leaves and the roots.
Nutritive powders are squeezed
From unheard of grasses and shoots.
I draw the line at my bread
They've loaded with three kinds of seeds,
Wheat germ and hard-shelled type grains
To bolster my vitamin needs.
The kernels get stuck in my teeth,
The crunching and chomping's absurd—
If munching on seeds were my fate
Then God would have made me a bird!

— Catherine Mary Weidum

Vegetable Pudding

This is a little different, but good!

- 1 cup ground carrots, about 3 large
- 1 cup peeled, ground potatoes
- 1 cup peeled, ground apples
- • dash nutmeg
- 1 cup granulated sugar
- 1 cup flour
- 1 tsp. salt
- 1 tsp. baking powder
- 1 tsp. soda
- 1 tsp. cinnamon
- 1 egg
- 2 Tbsps. melted butter
- 1 cup raisins
- • pineapple and cherries for garnish, if desired

Place carrots, potatoes, and apples in a large bowl. Sift together nutmeg, granulated sugar, flour, salt, baking powder, soda, and cinnamon; add to bowl with vegetables and mix.

Add egg, melted butter and raisins. Blend well. Pour into well-buttered 2-quart casserole and bake at 300° for about 2 hours. Garnish with pineapple and cherries, if desired. Makes 12 servings.

Violet Beard
Marshall, Illinois
May 22, 1990

Tuna Cauliflower Fiesta

This company casserole is as colorful as confetti and good for buffet service.

- 2 7-oz. cans chunk-style tuna
- 2 10-oz. pkgs. frozen cauliflower
- ¼ cup green pepper strips
- ¼ cup tuna oil OR salad oil
- ¼ cup flour
- ½ tsp. salt
- ⅛ tsp. pepper
- 1½ cups milk
- ¼ cup pimento strips
- ⅔ cup grated Cheddar cheese

Drain tuna, reserving oil. Cook cauliflower until just tender-crisp, drain. Place in well-greased 2-quart casserole. Layer tuna chunks over cauliflower. Cook green pepper in oil until tender; blend in flour and seasonings. Add milk and cook until thickened, stirring constantly. Add pimento; pour sauce over tuna. Top with cheese. Bake in 350° oven 35 minutes. Makes 6 servings.

Elizabeth McJunkin
Toronto, Kansas
June 18, 1991

Reunion Scalloped Potatoes

This recipe will serve 20 people; ideal for a get-together.

5   lbs. potatoes, boiled in jackets, peeled and sliced
1   small can pimento, finely cut
1   small onion, finely diced
¼   lb. butter OR margarine
1   Tbsp. flour
1   tsp. salt
1   10½-oz. can cream of mushroom soup
1   cup milk
1   lb. cheese, shredded

Arrange potatoes in a buttered baking dish. Combine the remaining ingredients in a saucepan and stir over low heat until blended and cheese is melted. Pour over the potatoes. Bake in 300° oven for 1½ hours.

Mrs. Orlin Petersen
Utica, South Dakota
June 20, 1989

Swiss Green Bean Casserole

Cooked fresh green beans could be used in this recipe.

2   15½-16 oz. cans whole green beans, drained
1   8-oz. carton french onion dip
2   Tbsps. margarine
2   Tbsps. flour
2   Tbsps. milk
¼   lb. Swiss cheese, grated
•   paprika

Melt margarine in a small heavy saucepan, add flour and stir until smooth. Add onion dip and milk, stirring until smooth. Layer beans and ⅔ of sauce in a 1½-quart lightly buttered casserole. Top with cheese. Pour remaining sauce over all. Sprinkle with paprika. Cover and bake in 325° oven for 20 minutes or until cheese melts. Makes 8 servings.

Rose M. Dietz
Hoisington, Kansas
September 11, 1990

Chiffon Sweet Potato Pie

The humble sweet potato pie is fit for a king when it is made this way!

2   **eggs, separated**
½   **cup molasses**
¼   **tsp. nutmeg**
¼   **tsp. cinnamon**
½   **tsp. salt**
1   **cup mashed sweet potatoes**
½   **cup milk**
½   **cup orange gelatin powder**
¼   **cup cold water**
½   **cup honey**
½   **cup whipping cream**
1   **9-inch baked pastry shell**
¾   **cup pecan halves, optional**

Mix together in top of double boiler: egg yolks, molasses, nutmeg, cinnamon, salt and sweet potatoes. Stir in milk and cook over boiling water until thick, stirring frequently. Dissolve gelatin in water and add to first mixture. Cook until well blended.

Remove from heat. Beat egg whites stiff, but not dry. Gradually beat honey into egg whites. Fold egg white mixture into first mixture.

Pour combined mixture into baked pie shell. Place in refrigerator. Just before serving, spread lightly sweetened whipped cream over pie.

If a more elaborate pie is desired, place ½ cup of broken pecan meats in bottom of pie shell before filling it and decorate top of pie with pecan halves.

Mrs. I. B. Flint
Lincoln, Nebraska
September 24, 1957

■ Creative Cooks ■

Creative cooks, like you and me,
disdain to follow a recipe.
We cook by instinct and with flair,
make substitutions here and there,
use different spices, methods, tools;
bend, and often break, the rules.
So, when one of our inspired creations
brings raves from guests and near relations,
heart-warming praise and cries of "More!"
What do we do for an encore?
Say we've lost the recipe, or hid it.
Or admit we've forgotten how we did it?

— R.H. Grenville

Broccoli Puff

I think you will like this recipe.

2   10-oz. pkgs. chopped broccoli
3   eggs, separated
1   Tbsp. flour
•   pinch of ground nutmeg
1   cup mayonnaise
1   Tbsp. butter OR margarine, softened
¼   tsp. salt
¼   tsp. pepper
¼   cup PLUS 1 Tbsp. Parmesan cheese

Cook broccoli and drain well. Beat egg yolks; add flour, mixing well. Stir in nutmeg, mayonnaise, margarine, salt, pepper and cheese. Add broccoli, mixing lightly.

Beat egg whites (room temperature) until stiff, but not dry; gently fold into broccoli mixture. Pour into lightly buttered 9-inch square baking dish. Bake in 350° oven for 30-40 minutes or until browned and set.

Tamra Boyce
Anoka, Minnesota
January 1, 1991

Danish Limas

This is a wonderful way to serve lima beans.

2   10-oz. pkgs. frozen lima beans
½   cup diced celery
¼   cup chopped onion
1   cup sour cream
½   cup crumbled blue cheese
¼   cup chopped pimento
4   slices of fried bacon

In saucepan, cook limas, celery and onion in boiling water until tender. Drain well. Stir in blue cheese and sour cream. Cook and stir over low heat until cheese has melted; do not boil. Stir in pimento. Turn into serving dish and sprinkle crumbled bacon on top.

Della B. Craft
Osawatomie, Kansas
September 25, 1990

Curried Bean and Rice Salad

Excellent any time of year.

2 cups cooked rice
• chicken broth
1½ cups drained red kidney beans
½ cup celery
2 green onions, chopped
2 Tbsps. green pepper
2 Tbsps. slivered almonds
1 Tbsp. lime juice
½ tsp. curry powder
½ cup mayonnaise
• salt
• pepper
• tomatoes
• parsley

Cook rice in chicken broth. Combine with beans, celery, onions, green pepper, almonds, lime juice, curry powder and mayonnaise. Add salt and pepper to taste. Mix well and marinate overnight. Decorate salad with wedges of tomatoes and parsley.

Ellen Christiansen
Palos Verdes Peninsula,
California
April 24, 1990

Corn Bread Salad

This is one of my favorite salads.

1 8x8-inch pan of corn bread, crumbled
8 green onions with tops, chopped
8 radishes, chopped
½ green bell pepper, chopped
2 tomatoes, chopped
¼ cup mayonnaise
¼ cup cucumber salad dressing
2 tsps. prepared mustard

Combine corn bread, onions, radishes, pepper and tomatoes. Mix mayonnaise, dressing and mustard. Pour over corn bread and vegetables and toss.

Carolyn Steward
Collinsville, Oklahoma
April 13, 1993

Thai Chicken and Vegetable Salad

A Pillsbury BAKE-OFF winner.

Salad:
2   Tbsps. oil
2   whole chicken breasts, skinned, boned, cut into 2x¼-inch strips
¼   tsp. garlic salt
1   16-oz. pkg. frozen broccoli-carrot combination
8   cups shredded lettuce
½   cup fresh bean sprouts
⅓   cup thinly sliced green onions
•   tomato wedges
•   fresh cilantro

Dressing:
¾   cup oil
¼   cup rice wine vinegar OR white vinegar
2   Tbsps. soy sauce
2   Tbsps. peanut butter
¼-½ tsp. cayenne pepper
2   garlic cloves, minced

In blender container or food processor bowl with metal blade, combine all dressing ingredients. Cover, blend until smooth. Set aside.

Heat 1 tablespoon of the oil in large skillet over medium-high heat. Add chicken; stir-fry about 5 minutes or until no longer pink. Remove from skillet; sprinkle chicken with garlic salt. Add remaining 1 tablespoon oil to skillet. Add frozen vegetables; stir-fry for 5-7 minutes or until vegetables are crisp-tender.

Place 2 cups of the shredded lettuce on each of 4 serving plates. Top each with ¼ of the bean sprouts, green onions, cooked vegetables and cooked chicken. Spoon dressing over each salad. Garnish with tomatoes and cilantro. Serve with remaining dressing. Serve warm or cold. Makes 4 servings.

Kate Marchbanks Food Story
June 5, 1990

Fruited Chicken Salad

1½ cups chopped, cooked chicken OR turkey
1 cup apple, unpeeled and chopped
¾ cup celery, chopped
½ cup walnuts, chopped
1 3-oz. pkg. cream cheese, softened
3 Tbsps. pineapple juice
¼ tsp. salt
⅛ tsp. white pepper

Combine chicken or turkey, apple, celery and walnuts. Combine cream cheese, pineapple juice, salt and white pepper, mixing well. Add cream cheese mixture to chicken mixture, stirring well. Cover and chill. Makes 6 servings.

Jeanie Blass
Richmond, Virginia
August 16, 1994

Shoestring Salad

A filling salad that's different.

1 cup shredded carrots
1 cup diced celery
2 Tbsps. minced onion
½ cup salad dressing
2 Tbsps. milk
1 can chicken OR tuna, drained
1 can shoestring potatoes

Mix first 5 ingredients. Just before serving, add canned chicken or tuna and shoestring potatoes. Serve on lettuce.

Polly Williams
Hurst, Texas
May 10, 1994

You Won't Believe It Isn't Potato Salad

This is really amazing!

45 soda crackers
3 hard-boiled eggs
½ cup celery
½ cup green pepper
¼ cup dill pickle
¼ cup sweet pickle
¼ cup stuffed olives
¼ onion
¼ cup radishes
1 tsp. dry mustard
1 8-oz. jar mayonnaise

Crumble crackers. Chop eggs, celery, green pepper, pickles, olives, onion and radishes. Add dry mustard and crumbled crackers. Mix thoroughly. Add mayonnaise and mix again. Refrigerate 1 hour before serving.

Lillian Stewart
Paris, Illinois
July 17, 1990

Beet Salad

This is good any time with any kind of meat.

1 pkg. cherry gelatin
1 pkg. strawberry gelatin
1 pkg. raspberry gelatin
3 cups hot water
½ cup sweet pickle juice
1 can shoestring beets OR chopped beets
1 large can crushed pineapple
1 cup salad dressing
1 cup chopped celery
½ cup chopped green onion

Dissolve the 3 packages of gelatin in the hot water. Add juice, beets and pineapple to hot gelatin and pour into a 9x13-inch pan. Refrigerate.

Mix salad dressing, celery and green onion together and spread on top of set gelatin. Cut into squares to serve.

Mrs. Howard Seaver
Raymond, South Dakota
April 9, 1991

Broccoli Salad

I'm sure you'll like this delicious salad.

4   cups chopped broccoli
1   cup raisins
1   cup shelled sunflower seeds
½   cup chopped sweet onion
6-8 slices cooked bacon, broken up

Dressing:
1   cup mayonnaise
¼   cup granulated sugar
1   Tbsp. vinegar

Combine broccoli (I use just the heads), raisins, seeds, onion and bacon pieces. Mix together mayonnaise, granulated sugar and vinegar. Pour dressing over broccoli mixture.

Ruth Rendall
Bricelyn, Minnesota
March 3, 1992

Greengage Plum Salad

This salad will make any meat taste better.

1   3-oz. pkg. lime gelatin
1½ cups hot water
½   cup plum syrup
¼   tsp. salt
1   tsp. vinegar
1   No. 2½ can greengage plums
½   cup slivered almonds
¼   tsp. dry ginger
2   3-oz. pkgs. cream cheese

Dissolve gelatin in hot water. Add syrup, salt and vinegar and cool. Cut fruit from pits and place in mold. Scatter nuts over plums and cover with half the gelatin. Chill until firm. Chill remaining half of gelatin in separate bowl until partially set. Beat with rotary beater, then add ginger and softened cream cheese. Pour over other half of gelatin and chill. Serve on lettuce with a fruit dressing if desired.

Mrs. Orlin Petersen
Utica, South Dakota
April 11, 1989

Polynesian Coleslaw

This is one of our favorites.

1   8-oz. can pineapple tidbits
½   cup mayonnaise OR salad dressing
4   cups shredded cabbage
¼   tsp. white pepper
¼   tsp. ground ginger
¼   tsp. ground nutmeg
1   11-oz. can mandarin oranges, drained

Drain pineapple, reserving 2 tablespoons liquid. Combine liquid with mayonnaise. Combine cabbage, seasonings and mayonnaise in large bowl. Add pineapple and mandarin oranges. Toss gently. Cover and chill. Makes 6 servings.

Mrs. E. O'Brien
Richmond, Virginia
August 27, 1991

Broccoli-Cauliflower Salad

This is a delicious salad recipe that can be taken to club meetings or potlucks. Let me warn you: Take the recipe with you.

1   head of broccoli
1   head of cauliflower
1   medium red onion, diced
1   cup grated cheese
½   lb. bacon, fried

Dressing:
¾   cup salad dressing
¼   cup granulated sugar or 3 packets artificial sweetener
3   Tbsps. wine vinegar

Cut broccoli and cauliflower into small pieces and combine with onion and cheese. Refrigerate.

Mix dressing and refrigerate. Cut bacon into small pieces.

When ready to serve, add crisp bacon and dressing to chilled mixture.

Mrs. P.L. Newingham
Pontiac, Michigan
June 19, 1990

■ Bran New Year ■

We know we should eat oat bran,
And now the New Year's here;
What better time to get resolve
With midnight drawing near?
So for our New Year's resolutions,
This is what we'll do:
Ring out the old;
Ring in the bran new.

— Sylvia Kreng

Carrot-Chive Salad

Brilliant colors, marvelous flavors!

½ cup salad oil
¼ cup vinegar
¼ tsp. salt
1 tsp. dried chives
2 Tbsps. syrup drained from canned pineapple
3 cups coarsely shredded carrots
1 13½-oz. can pineapple tidbits

Mix oil, vinegar, salt, chives and pineapple syrup. Mix carrots and drained pineapple tidbits, pour the oil-vinegar mixture over the top. Toss lightly. Chill at least 4 hours. Serve in shallow bowl. Makes 6-8 servings.

Elizabeth McJunkin
Toronto, Kansas
September 11, 1990

Artichoke Salad

A variety of vegetables and rice combine flavors in this chilled dish.

1 4-oz. jar artichokes
1 cup garbanzo beans
1 ripe avocado, peeled
2 Tbsps. vegetable oil
1 tsp. lemon juice
1 cup cold cooked rice
½ cup diced red pepper
½ cup diced green pepper
¼ cup diced onion
1 ripe tomato, chopped and seeded
• salt and pepper to taste
• lettuce leaves
• fresh parsley for garnish

Drain artichokes and beans. Dice avocado. In medium bowl, combine oil and lemon juice. Combine artichokes, beans, avocado, oil and lemon juice, rice, red and green pepper, onion, tomato and salt and pepper. Mix well. Chill, then serve on lettuce leaves on chilled plates, garnished with parsley. Makes 4 servings.

Linda Hutton
Decatur, Illinois
May 24, 1994

Spinach-Orange Salad

This is a light, refreshing salad.

1 6-oz. bag fresh spinach
1 medium onion, diced
1 green pepper, diced
1 cucumber, sliced
1 16-oz. can mandarin oranges, drained
¾ cup mayonnaise
2 Tbsps. honey
1 Tbsp. lemon juice
2 Tbsps. caraway seeds

Rinse and stem spinach. Dry spinach and tear into bite-sized pieces. Toss with onion, pepper, cucumber and oranges. To make dressing, mix mayonnaise, honey, lemon juice and caraway seed. Pour over salad.

Pat Habiger
Spearville, Kansas
September 26, 1989

Asparagus Salad

I think this is very good and different!

1 10½-oz. can cream of asparagus soup
1 8-oz. pkg. cream cheese
1 3-oz. pkg. lemon gelatin
1 cup boiling water
½ tsp. lemon flavoring
1 1-lb. can asparagus, drained, OR 1 cup fresh asparagus, cooked and drained
½ cup diced celery
½ cup diced green pepper
2 tsps. minced onion
2 tsps. minced pimento
½ cup finely chopped pecans
½ cup mayonnaise

Heat and stir the asparagus soup and cream cheese until well blended. Dissolve gelatin in boiling water; add flavoring. Cool and add the asparagus, celery, green pepper, onion, pimento, pecans and mayonnaise. Stir in the soup-cheese mixture. Pour into a mold or an 8x10-inch glass dish. Chill until firm.

Mrs. H. Buettner
Bode, Iowa
July 17, 1984

Rice Fruit Salad

This salad can be refrigerated for several days.

1   cup vanilla ice cream
⅓ cup granulated sugar
1   tsp. salt
2   cups cooked rice, cooled
1   17-oz. can fruit cocktail
1   cup shredded coconut
1   cup pecans, broken
⅛ tsp. lemon juice
⅓ cup maraschino cherries

Combine ice cream, granulated sugar and salt; beat until soft. Fold in rice, fruit cocktail, coconut, pecans and lemon juice. Arrange cherries on top. Chill well, do not freeze.

Ruth Bryant
Decatur, Illinois
January 16, 1990

Sweet-Sour Cabbage

Grandma's recipe makes a splendid dish served hot with corned beef, boiled tongue or short ribs.

3   cups shredded cabbage (red cabbage preferred)
2   diced, unpeeled red apples
¼ cup vinegar
¼ cup water
¼ cup brown sugar
2   Tbsps. bacon fat
1   tsp. salt
½ tsp. caraway seed
½ tsp. celery seed

Cook all ingredients in uncovered saucepan for 30 minutes, stirring frequently. Serve hot.

Mamie Fly
Wichita, Kansas
March 17, 1959

Summer Green Bean Salad

2   lbs. fresh, young, tender green beans, trimmed but left whole
½   cup salad oil
¼   cup red wine vinegar
3   shallots, peeled and chopped fine
1   Tbsp. finely chopped parsley
•   salt and pepper to taste

Bring a large pot of water to boil. Add green beans and cook 6-8 minutes or until crisp-tender. Don't overcook or they'll lose their bright color and crisp texture. Drain and refresh under cold water. Wrap beans in paper towels to absorb moisture; put in large bowl. In a small bowl, blend oil, vinegar, shallots, parsley, salt and pepper. Pour over green beans and shake bowl to distribute dressing. Cover and refrigerate until ready to use.

Mrs. Harriet Bien
Rome, New York
August 1, 1989

Tomato Aspic Extraordinaire

1   Tbsp. dry onion soup mix
1   cup boiling water
1   3-oz. pkg. lemon gelatin
1   cup cold spaghetti sauce

Dissolve the soup mix in boiling water. Empty gelatin into a large bowl and add the water-onion liquid. Add the spaghetti sauce and mix well. Pour into decorative bowl or mold. Chill until set. Makes 4-6 servings.

Mrs. Deena Fisher
Toronto, Ontario, Canada
August 1, 1989

Mouth-Watering Cakes

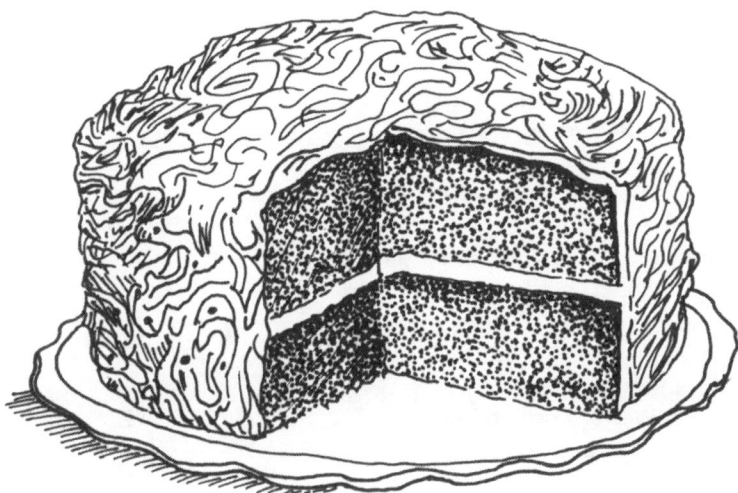

■ Mouth-Watering Cakes ■

Three-in-One Chocolate Torte 107
Rhubarb Custard Cake 107
Rhubarb Coffeecake 108
Apple Pie Cake 108
Blueberry Poppy Seed Brunch Cake 109
Cherry Chocolate Cake 110
Moist Banana Bundt Cake 110
Chocolate Praline Layer Cake 111
Strawberry Soda Pop Cake 112
Black Walnut Cake 113
Chocolate Carrot Cake 113
Punch Bowl Cake 114
Champagne Cake 114
Chocolate Eclair Cake 115
My Ranch Cake 116
Mississippi Mud Cake 117
Hawaiian Pineapple Poke Cake 118
Raisin Lemon Cake 118
Miniature Cheesecakes 119
Brown Sugar Meringue Spice Cake 119
Chocolate-Caramel Poke and Pour Cake 120
Filled Cupcakes 120
Cholesterol-Free Lemon Chiffon Cake 121
Yuletide Eggnog Cake 122
Chocolate Beet Cake 123
Coke Cake with Icing 123
Cranberry Coffeecake 124
Grandma West's Chocolate Cake 125
Cherry Cheesecake 125
Best Rhubarb Shortcake 126
Baby Food Cake 126
Prince of Wales Cake 127
Unusual Frozen Cake 127
Poppy Seed Cake 128
Mexican Chocolate Chiffon Cake 129
Blueberry Surprise Cake 129
Snow Mountain Cake 130
Vanilla Wafer Cake 131
Skillet Apple Cake 131
Caramel Pecan Cheesecake 132
Sock-it-to-me Cake 132
Black Forest Cake 133
Orange Dessert Cake 134
Cold Oven Pound Cake 134
Pumpkin Pie Cake 135
Rich and Delicious Cake 135

Three-in-One Chocolate Torte

This is one of our family cakes that doesn't last long.

Cake:
- 1 pkg. German chocolate cake mix

Chocolate syrup:
- 1 heaping Tbsp. cocoa
- 2 Tbsps. butter
- ¾ cup granulated sugar
- ⅓ cup milk

Frosting:
- 1 8-oz. pkg. light cream cheese
- ⅔ cup granulated sugar
- ⅓ cup chocolate syrup, cooled
- 2 cups whipped topping

Prepare cake mix as directed. Pour into two 8x8-inch pans and bake at 350° for 35-40 minutes or until done. Cool cake.

Make syrup by boiling cocoa, butter, ¾ cup granulated sugar and milk until smooth and melted; about 4 minutes. Cool.

Mix cream cheese, ⅔ cup granulated sugar, and ⅓ cup of the chocolate syrup; fold whipped topping into mixture. Spread frosting between cake layers. Drizzle chocolate syrup over top and let run down sides of cake. Refrigerate.

Arleen Young
North Platte, Nebraska
January 4, 1994

Rhubarb Custard Cake

The fruit and custard sink to the bottom during baking and form a nice custard layer.

- 1 yellow cake mix
- 5 cups rhubarb, diced
- 1½ cups granulated sugar
- 2 cups whipping cream (not whipped) OR half-and-half

Mix cake mix according to package directions. Pour into 9x13-inch pan. Mix rhubarb and granulated sugar together; sprinkle over cake mix batter. Pour whipping cream or half-and-half over all.

Bake at 350° for 45-55 minutes or until done.

Marlys Ratliff
West Alexandria, Ohio
June 7, 1994

Rhubarb Coffeecake

This is a very good recipe for using rhubarb.

1½   cups granulated
       sugar
½   cup shortening
1   egg
1   tsp. vanilla
1   cup sour milk
2½   cups flour
1½   tsps. baking soda
1   tsp. salt
2   cups diced rhubarb
1   cup brown sugar
1   tsp. cinnamon

Cream granulated sugar, shortening, egg and vanilla. Add milk, flour, baking soda and salt. Stir in rhubarb. Put in greased 9x13-inch pan. Sprinkle with brown sugar and cinnamon. Bake 30 minutes at 350°.

Lillie Kay
Grand Island, Nebraska
June 21, 1994

Apple Pie Cake

This tasty cake is quick to make when unexpected company comes.

1   cup granulated
       sugar
¼   cup butter
1   egg
1   cup sifted flour
¼   tsp. salt
1   tsp. nutmeg
1   tsp. cinnamon
1   tsp. baking soda
½   cup nuts (optional)
2½   cups diced apples
1   tsp. vanilla
2   Tbsps. hot water

Cream granulated sugar and butter; mix in egg. Sift together flour, salt, nutmeg, cinnamon and baking soda. Add to creamed mixture. Stir in nuts, apples, vanilla and water. Pour into greased 9-inch pie pan. Bake at 350° for 45 minutes. Top with whipped cream or ice cream to serve.

Marcella Schutter
Titonka, Iowa
October 11, 1994

Blueberry Poppy Seed Brunch Cake

This Grand Prize winner in the 1990 Pillsbury Bake-Off is baked in a springform pan.

Cake:
- ⅔ cup granulated sugar
- ½ cup butter OR margarine, softened
- 2 tsps. grated lemon peel
- 1 egg
- 1½ cups all-purpose OR unbleached flour
- 2 Tbsps. poppy seeds
- ½ tsp. baking soda
- ¼ tsp. salt
- ½ cup dairy sour cream

Filling:
- 2 cups fresh OR frozen blueberries, thawed, drained on paper towel
- ⅓ cup granulated sugar
- 2 tsps. flour
- ¼ tsp. nutmeg

Glaze:
- ⅓ cup powdered sugar
- 1-2 tsps. milk

Heat oven to 350°. Grease and flour bottom and sides of 9- or 10-inch springform pan. In large bowl, beat ⅔ cup granulated sugar and butter until light and fluffy. Add lemon peel and egg; beat 2 minutes at medium speed. Lightly spoon flour into measuring cup; level off. In medium bowl, combine 1½ cups flour, poppy seeds, baking soda and salt; add butter mixture alternately with sour cream. Spread batter over bottom and 1 inch up sides of greased and floured pan, making sure batter on sides is ¼-inch thick.

In medium bowl, combine all filling ingredients; spoon over batter. Bake at 350° for 45-55 minutes or until crust is golden brown. Cool slightly. Remove sides of pan.

In small bowl, combine powdered sugar and enough milk until glaze is of desired drizzling consistency; blend until smooth. Drizzle over top of warm cake. Serve warm or cool. Makes 8 servings.

**Kate Marchbanks Food Story
March 27, 1990**

Cherry Chocolate Cake

There are many variations to this recipe. Try applesauce cake mix with a raisin pie filling; yellow cake mix with peach pie filling; orange cake mix with pineapple filling; gingerbread mix with mincemeat pie filling, etc.

1   chocolate cake mix (two-layer size)
1   21-oz. can cherry pie filling
1   Tbsp. almond extract
2   eggs

Combine all ingredients and mix by hand until thoroughly combined. Pour into a plastic or glass Bundt pan, well greased. Pan may be sprinkled lightly with granulated sugar before adding batter. Let the batter stand 8-10 minutes. Then microwave on HIGH for about 12-14 minutes. Test for doneness with toothpick. Cake must be turned occasionally to allow even baking. Let cool 5 minutes before removing from pan. Serve with whipped topping or sprinkle with powdered sugar.

Florine Horst
Loveland, Colorado
April 26, 1983

Moist Banana Bundt Cake

One day I was doing some experimenting and came up with this. My husband and 2 older girls love the cake. My 9-month-old daughter even said: "Mum-m-m!"

5   medium overripe bananas
¼   cup hot water
3   tsps. soda
3   eggs
2   cups granulated sugar
2   sticks margarine, softened
1   tsp. vanilla
2   cups flour
1   cup nuts, chopped

In blender add bananas, hot water, and soda. Mix until a thick liquid forms.

In large bowl, beat eggs; add granulated sugar, margarine and vanilla. Beat on medium speed 2 minutes. Add flour and banana mixtures alternately. Add nuts. Bake in well-greased Bundt pan at 350° for 70 minutes.

F. Carr
Satanta, Kansas
April 24, 1984

110

Chocolate Praline Layer Cake

A Pillsbury BAKE-OFF winner.

Cake:
- ½ **cup butter OR margarine**
- ¼ **cup whipping cream**
- 1 **cup firmly packed brown sugar**
- ¾ **cup coarsely chopped pecans**
- 1 **pkg. pudding-included devil's food cake mix**
- 1¼ **cups water**
- ⅓ **cup oil**
- 3 **eggs**

Topping:
- 1¾ **cups whipping cream**
- ¼ **cup powdered sugar**
- ¼ **tsp. vanilla**
- • **whole pecans, if desired**
- • **chocolate curls, if desired**

In small heavy saucepan, combine butter, ¼ cup whipping cream and brown sugar. Cook over low heat just until butter is melted, stirring occasionally. Pour into two 9- or 8-inch round cake pans, sprinkle evenly with chopped pecans. In large bowl combine cake mix, water, oil and eggs at low speed until moistened; beat 2 minutes at highest speed. Carefully spoon batter over pecan mixture.

Bake in preheated 325° oven for 35-45 minutes or until cake springs back when touched lightly in center. Cool 5 minutes. Remove from pans. Cool completely.

In small bowl, beat 1¾ cups whipping cream until soft peaks form. Blend in powdered sugar and vanilla; beat until stiff peaks form. To assemble cake, place 1 layer on serving plate, praline side up. Spread with ½ of whipped cream. Top with second layer, praline side up; spread top with remaining whipped cream. Garnish with whole pecans and chocolate curls, if desired. Store in refrigerator. Makes 12 servings.

**Kate Marchbanks Food Story
March 15, 1988**

Strawberry Soda Pop Cake

My grandma used to make this cake years ago.

Cake:
- ¾ cup shortening
- 2 cups granulated sugar
- 1 7-oz. bottle strawberry soda pop
- 3 cups flour
- 2 tsps. baking powder
- ½ tsp. salt
- 1 cup chopped nuts (optional)
- 5 egg whites, stiffly beaten

Frosting:
- 2 Tbsps. soft shortening
- • pinch of salt
- 2 cups powdered sugar
- • strawberry soda pop, to moisten

For cake, cream together shortening and granulated sugar. After sifting flour, baking powder and salt together, add soda pop alternately with dry ingredients. Add nuts. Fold in egg whites. Bake in 3 layers or a 10x14-inch pan at 350° for 30-40 minutes.

For frosting, combine shortening, salt, powdered sugar and enough soda pop to moisten. (Or use strawberry jam between layers instead of frosting.)

Editor's Note: Because she believes that today's strawberry soda pop is lacking the full-bodied flavor of yesteryear's, Mrs. Wohler suggests adding ¼ teaspoon strawberry flavoring to the mix. She says that this makes a better tasting and prettier cake.

Wilma Wohler
Brookville, Kansas
September 27, 1994

■ The Old Crock ■

I bought this crock at a yard sale,
And, well, you may laugh.
I got it because it reminded me
Of the one we used in the past.
How good the milk tasted
When dipped from that old crock,
How rich, luscious, and golden,
The Jersey cream floating on top.
Those days are long gone;
They'll never come again.
I'll plant a flower in my crock
And cherish the memories that remain.

— Ruth Owens

Black Walnut Cake

If you've hulled and picked your walnuts, now is a good time to make this delicious cake.

- ⅔ cup margarine OR shortening
- 1½ cups granulated sugar
- 1 tsp. vanilla
- ¼ tsp. almond extract
- ⅛ tsp. salt
- 3 cups flour
- 3 tsps. baking powder
- 1¼ cups milk
- ¼ cup black walnuts, chopped
- 4 egg whites, beaten

Cream shortening and granulated sugar. Add flavorings, salt, flour, baking powder and milk. Beat 2 minutes. Fold in nuts and egg whites. Pour into 2 layer cake pans, greased and floured or lined with waxed paper.

Bake 30 minutes in a moderately slow oven (about 325°). Cool and frost. Seven-minute frosting or coconut frosting is very good with this cake.

Esther Herman
Riverton, Nebraska
November 18, 1975

Chocolate Carrot Cake

- 1¾ cups all-purpose flour
- ½ cup cocoa
- 1 tsp. baking powder
- ½ tsp. baking soda
- • dash of salt
- ½ cup granulated sugar
- 1 cup brown sugar
- 1 tsp. cinnamon
- 1¼ cups melted butter
- 3 eggs
- 2 cups grated carrots, about 2 large
- ⅓ cup raisins

Chocolate Cream Cheese Frosting:
- ¼ cup butter, softened
- 1 8-oz. pkg. cream cheese, softened
- 1 cup powdered sugar
- 3 Tbsps. cocoa

Stir together in a large bowl: flour, cocoa, baking powder, soda, salt, cinnamon and sugars. Beat together eggs and melted butter with electric mixer. Combine mixture with dry ingredients. By hand, stir in carrots and raisins. Grease and flour two 8-inch cake pans; divide cake batter between them. Bake in 350° oven for 25-30 minutes or until cake tester comes out clean.

To make frosting, beat together butter and cream cheese in a small mixing bowl. Beat in powdered sugar and cocoa until well blended. Spread evenly on both layers of cake.

Beverly Wilkins
Scarsborough, Ontario, Canada
June 20, 1989

Punch Bowl Cake

This makes a showy dessert!

1   yellow cake mix, prepared according to pkg. directions
2   pkgs. instant vanilla pudding
2-3 bananas (enough to cover layers)
1   16-oz. can crushed pineapple
2   cartons frozen strawberries
2   8-oz. cartons whipped topping
•   pecan halves

Bake 2-layer cake as directed. To assemble in punch bowl, place 1 layer in bottom of bowl. Prepare instant pudding. Use half on first layer. Slice bananas over top of pudding. Pour ½ can pineapple (juice and all) over bananas. Put strawberries ¼-inch deep over pineapple. Top with 1 carton whipped topping. Beginning with second cake, repeat all layers. Top with pecan halves. Refrigerate.

Mrs. Earvie Weller
Belle, Missouri
December 9, 1986

Champagne Cake

This is a very popular cake now.

1   pkg. Jiffy cake mix, yellow OR white, prepared according to pkg. directions
1   8-oz. pkg. cream cheese
1   small box instant vanilla pudding and pie mix
1½ cups milk
1   20-oz. can crushed pineapple, drained
1   small container whipped topping

Prepare cake mix as directed on package, and pour batter into a greased and floured 9x13-inch pan. Bake 15 minutes at temperature on the box. Let cool.

Beat cream cheese until very soft. Blend pudding mix and milk into cream cheese. Spread over top of cooled cake. Spread drained pineapple over cream cheese mixture. Top with whipped topping.

Carolyn S. Webb
Versailles, Missouri
November 19, 1991

114

Chocolate Eclair Cake

I love to share this recipe with people who want something different, something easy to make, which doesn't cost much to make and is a delight to eat!

Filling:
- graham crackers (enough to line 9x13-inch pan, twice)
- 1   6-oz. pkg. OR two 3-oz. pkgs. French vanilla pudding mix
- 3   cups milk
- 1   8-oz. container whipped topping

Frosting:
- 1   cup granulated sugar
- ⅓   cup cocoa
- ¼   cup milk
- ¼   cup butter OR margarine
- 1   tsp. vanilla

To make filling: Butter a 9x13-inch pan and line bottom with whole graham crackers, being careful not to crack them. Combine pudding mix in bowl with milk and whipped topping. Pour a layer of the pudding mixture over graham crackers; then put another layer of the graham crackers over the pudding. Refrigerate while preparing the frosting.

To make frosting: Combine granulated sugar, cocoa and milk in a pan with a thick bottom. Bring to a boil over medium heat, being very careful not to burn. When mixture comes to a rolling boil, cook for 1 minute. Remove from heat and add butter or margarine and vanilla. Cool. (Place pan in cold water to speed cooling, if desired.) Beat until mixture starts to thicken enough to spread it on top of graham crackers. Refrigerate overnight or a day ahead. Cut into serving pieces.

Mary Wallace
Nora Springs, Iowa
March 29, 1994

115

My Ranch Cake

- 1½ cups boiling water
- 1 cup uncooked quick oatmeal
- 1 stick butter OR margarine
- 1½ cups flour
- 1 tsp. soda
- 1½ tsps. cinnamon
- ½ tsp. salt
- 1 cup MINUS 2 Tbsps. granulated sugar
- 1 cup packed brown sugar
- 2 beaten eggs

Topping:
- ¾ cup packed brown sugar
- 2 Tbsps. milk
- 6 Tbsps. butter OR margarine
- ½ cup pecans
- 1 cup coconut

Break butter into chunks and pour boiling water over oatmeal and butter. Stir until butter melts. Set aside. Sift flour, soda, cinnamon and salt and add to oat mixture. Mix well. Add both sugars. Add eggs. Mix thoroughly. Bake in greased 9x13-inch pan in preheated 375° oven for about 25 minutes.

To make topping: Combine brown sugar, milk and butter. Boil 1 minute then remove from heat. Blend in pecans and coconut and spread on warm cake. Place under broiler long enough to brown slightly.

Nadine Waldron
Walden, Colorado
May 10, 1988

■ Kitchen Things? Well ... ■

We have waffle irons and
common toasters,
ten and twenty gallon roasters,
not to mention kitchen pans
and hot pads to protect your hands,
everyday and china dishes,
special pans for cooking fishes,
preserving jars with rubber rings
and those little timer things.
We have blenders, scales,
knives, and slicers,

Mississippi Mud Cake

- 2 sticks (1 cup) margarine
- ½ cup unsweetened cocoa
- 2 cups granulated sugar
- 4 eggs, slightly beaten
- 1½ cups flour
- 1 tsp. vanilla
- ½ tsp. salt
- ½ tsp. baking soda
- 1½ cups chopped pecans
- • miniature marshmallows

Frosting:
- ⅓ cup milk
- ½ stick (¼ cup) margarine
- ⅓ cup cocoa
- 1 1-lb. box powdered sugar

Melt margarine with cocoa. Remove from heat and stir in granulated sugar and eggs, mixing well. Add flour, vanilla, salt and baking soda. Stir in pecans. Spoon batter into a greased and floured 9x13-inch pan. Bake in 350° oven for 35-40 minutes, or until cake tests done. Remove from oven.

Cover the top of the cake with miniature marshmallows while cake is still hot.

To make frosting, heat milk, margarine, cocoa and powdered sugar together. When cake is cool, frost it.

Mrs. Herbert Stearns
Avoca, Iowa
May 27, 1986

yogurt makers, veggie dicers,
glass and plastic mixing bowls,
colanders filled with empty holes.
We have pretty little ramekins,
assorted kinds of cupcake tins,
racks for pies and racks for rolls,
elegant dishes for casseroles,
crockery, pewter, and silver jugs,
eight and twelve ounce coffee mugs.
Anything else? Let me think.
Oh yes, of course, the kitchen sink.

— Roger F. Tripp

Hawaiian Pineapple Poke Cake

I got this recipe in California, and I have never eaten any cake like it—so yummy!

1   pkg. yellow cake mix
1   20-oz. can crushed pineapple, drained

Topping I:
1   8-oz. pkg. cream cheese, softened
1   3¾-oz. box instant vanilla pudding
1   cup cold milk

Topping II:
2   cups whipped topping
•   coconut OR chopped nuts

Bake cake according to package directions, using a 9x13-inch pan. Cool cake thoroughly. Punch large holes over top of cake using handle of wooden spoon. Pour drained pineapple over top and spread to cover (some will go in holes).

Combine cream cheese, pudding mix and milk and beat until thick enough to spread over pineapple. Spread whipped topping over first topping. Sprinkle coconut or chopped nuts over whipped topping. Refrigerate cake for 1 hour. Cut in squares to serve.

Edna M. Stacy
Waterloo, Iowa
March 30, 1982

Raisin Lemon Cake

This is an old, old recipe that Gram and I make often. It is not too sweet, sort of a coffee cake—and very delicious.

1   cup raisins
1   Tbsp. flour
1   cup butter OR margarine, softened
2   cups granulated sugar
5   eggs
2   cups flour
1   Tbsp. grated lemon rind
¼   tsp. nutmeg
•   powdered sugar

Chop raisins with an oiled knife and toss to coat with 1 tablespoon flour. Set aside. Cream butter and granulated sugar in large mixing bowl until fluffy. Add 3 eggs, 1 at a time, beating 1 minute after each addition. Add ¼ cup flour and mix well. Add lemon rind and nutmeg. Add remaining 2 eggs. Beat until mixture resembles texture of whipped cream. Stir in remaining flour all at once, mixing well until blended. Fold in raisins. Turn batter into well-buttered and floured 10-inch fluted tube or plain tube pan. Put in cold oven. Turn oven to 350°. Bake 50-55 minutes or until knife inserted in center comes out clean. Let cake stand 10 minutes in pan, then invert on rack and cool completely. Dust with powdered sugar.

E.J. Sertich
Hot Springs, Arkansas
September 26, 1989

Miniature Cheesecakes

These make a delightful addition to a tea tray. They can be baked ahead, frozen, thawed quickly and topped with pie filling for a fast dessert.

24 vanilla wafers
2   8-oz. pkgs. cream cheese, softened
¾   cup granulated sugar
2   eggs
1   Tbsp. lemon juice, fresh OR bottled
1   tsp. vanilla
1   20½-oz. can pie filling (peach, cherry OR blueberry)
1   carton whipped topping, thawed

Place foil cupcake liners in cupcake pans. Place a vanilla wafer in bottom of each liner. In small bowl, beat cream cheese, granulated sugar, eggs, lemon juice and vanilla until light and fluffy. Fill liners ¾ full with cheese mixture. Bake in preheated 375° oven for 15-20 minutes until set. Top each with a spoonful of pie filling and a spoonful of thawed whipped topping before serving.

Elsie Ryan
Cresco, Iowa
May 9, 1989

Brown Sugar Meringue Spice Cake

This is made in a loaf pan and is absolutely scrumptious!

1⅓ cups sifted flour
½   tsp. baking soda
½   tsp. baking powder
½   tsp. cloves
½   tsp. cinnamon
¼   tsp. salt
½   cup shortening
1½ cups brown sugar, divided
2   eggs, separated
½   cup sour milk OR buttermilk

Sift flour, soda, baking powder, cloves, cinnamon and salt together. Cream shortening until soft; gradually add 1 cup brown sugar; continue to cream until light and fluffy. Beat 1 whole egg and 1 egg yolk until light; add to sugar mixture and beat thoroughly. Add sifted dry ingredients to mixture alternating with the sour milk, beating after each addition until smooth. Turn into greased and lightly floured loaf pan. Prepare meringue as follows: Beat remaining 1 egg white until quite stiff; gradually add remaining ½ cup brown sugar and continue to beat at high speed. Spread meringue over cake batter. Sprinkle with nutmeats and bake in moderate 350° oven for 50 minutes.

Sue Pipkin
Baxter Springs, Kansas
February 14, 1989

Chocolate-Caramel Poke and Pour Cake

This is very good for the holidays!

1 German chocolate cake mix, prepared according to pkg. directions
1 can sweetened condensed milk
1 pt. jar (or 2 cups) caramel OR butterscotch ice cream topping mix
1 8-oz. carton whipped topping
2-3 Heath candy bars, crushed

Prepare cake as directed on package and bake in a 9x13-inch pan in 350° oven for 30-35 minutes. Remove from oven and poke holes in cake with a wooden spoon. Pour sweetened condensed milk into holes. Pour ice cream topping over the milk. Frost with the whipped topping. Sprinkle crushed candy over top. Refrigerate, then enjoy.

Mrs. Joe Navrkal
Clarkson, Nebraska
December 18, 1990

Filled Cupcakes

You won't need to frost these cupcakes!

3 cups flour
2 cups granulated sugar
½ cup cocoa
2 tsps. baking soda
1 tsp. salt
2 cups cold water
⅔ cup vegetable oil
2 tsps. vinegar
2 tsps. vanilla

Filling:
1 8-oz. pkg. softened cream cheese
1 egg, unbeaten
⅓ cup granulated sugar
⅛ tsp. salt
1 6-oz. pkg. chocolate chips

Sift flour, granulated sugar, cocoa, soda and salt together. Add cold water, oil, vinegar and vanilla. Mix well and fill paper-lined or greased and floured cupcake pans ½ full.
To make filling, combine cream cheese, egg, granulated sugar and salt. Stir in chips. Top each cupcake with 1 heaping teaspoon of filling. Bake in 350° oven for 25 minutes. Makes about 30 cupcakes.

Anna Mae Miller
Jamesport, Missouri
April 11, 1989

Cholesterol-Free Lemon Chiffon Cake

This is a wonderful cake!

5	large egg whites, room temperature
2	Tbsps. sifted powdered sugar
1½	cups (5¼ ozs.) sifted cake flour
1	cup granulated sugar
2	tsps. baking powder
¼	tsp. salt
½	cup vegetable oil OR corn oil
•	grated rind of 2 lemons
½	cup fresh-squeezed lemon juice

In a large bowl, using electric mixer, whip egg whites with powdered sugar until fluffy, but not dry. Set whites aside. In another bowl, sift flour and granulated sugar, baking powder and salt. Scoop out a well in center of the flour and add oil, lemon rind and juice. With medium speed on mixer, beat until well blended and smooth. Fold the batter into the whites. Spread solid shortening on bottom and sides of 9-inch tube pan and dust with flour. Pour batter into pan and bake in 350° oven for 35-40 minutes, or until lightly browned on top (should spring back to touch). Cool cake right side up in pan for 5 minutes. Invert onto wire rack and lift off the pan. Cool completely and ice, if desired.

Mrs. Irvin Metcalf
Bauxite, Arkansas
September 11, 1990

KEEPING CAKES FRESH
To keep frosted cakes fresh after slicing, pat plastic wrap against the cut surfaces. The wrap will stick to the frosting and help keep the cake moist. Cakes will keep a day or 2 at room temperature, preferable under a cake dome. Longer than that, a cake needs to be refrigerated. For best flavor and texture, bring cakes that have been refrigerated or frozen back to room temperature before serving.

Yuletide Eggnog Cake

½ cup butter OR margarine
1⅓ cups granulated sugar
2 large eggs
1 tsp. vanilla
1 tsp. rum flavoring
3 cups flour
2½ tsps. baking powder
¾ tsp. salt
1½ cups eggnog
2 Tbsps. water

Frosting:
3 Tbsps. eggnog
2 Tbsps. light corn syrup
½ tsp. rum flavoring
2¾ cups powdered sugar

Combine butter and granulated sugar; beat well. Add eggs, 1 at time, beating well after each addition. Blend in vanilla and 1 teaspoon flavoring.

Sift together flour, salt and baking powder. Add alternately to creamed mixture with 1½ cups eggnog and water. Pour into a well-greased and floured 10-inch tube pan. Bake at 350° for 50-55 minutes. Cool completely on wire rack.

To make frosting, combine 3 tablespoons eggnog, corn syrup and flavoring. Gradually add powdered sugar and beat to spreading consistency. Frost cake. Add red and green cherries to cake top if desired.

Mrs. A. Mayer
Richmond, Virginia
December 5, 1989

■ If Grandmother's Bowl Could Talk ■

How many dreams
went into the creams
of how many puddings and cakes ...

How many tears
came terribly near
to sprinkling nuts and dates?

How many sighs
would rustle and rise
from how many loaves of bread ...

How many prayers
did Grandma prepare
before they were finally said?

If Grandmother's bowl could tell us
through cracked and faded clay,
we'd be amazed at the love she made
in her kitchen every day.

— Carole Turner Johnston

Chocolate Beet Cake

This is a very good cake.

2 cups all-purpose flour
2 tsps. baking powder
½ tsp. salt
⅓ cup cocoa
3 eggs
1 cup granulated sugar
1 cup cooked, grated beets
½ cup corn oil
¼ cup orange juice
2 tsps. grated orange rind
1 tsp. vanilla extract
1 6-oz. pkg. semi-sweet chocolate morsels
• powdered sugar (optional)

Combine flour, baking powder, salt and cocoa; set aside. Combine eggs and granulated sugar in a large bowl, mixing well. Add beets, oil, orange juice and orange rind to sugar mixture. Beat well. Stir in flour mixture and vanilla. Mix well. Stir in chocolate morsels. Pour into greased 9-inch square baking pan. Bake in 350° oven for 40 minutes or until cake tests done. Let cool 10 minutes in pan, then remove and cool completely on wire rack. Sprinkle with powdered sugar if desired. Makes 16 servings.

Mrs. A. Mayer
Richmond, Virginia
September 2, 1980

Coke Cake with Icing

Here's a cake with a special flavor that will be a hit with Coke lovers everywhere.

1 cup soft margarine
2 cups flour
1¼ cups granulated sugar
3 Tbsps. cocoa
1 tsp. soda
1 tsp. vanilla
2 eggs
½ cup buttermilk
1 cup tiny marsh-mallows
1 cup Coke

Icing:
½ cup soft margarine
3 Tbsps. cocoa
⅓ cup Coke
4 cups powdered sugar
1 cup chopped, toasted pecans

Blend together in large mixer bowl margarine, flour, granulated sugar, cocoa, soda, vanilla, eggs and buttermilk. Add the cup of Coke and mix in the tiny marshmallows by hand. Pour into 9x13-inch greased and floured baking dish. Bake in 350° oven 40-45 minutes. Cool for 30 minutes and then frost the cake with its own special Coke frosting.
To make frosting, blend together margarine, cocoa, Coke and powdered sugar. Beat until smooth; add pecans. Spread on top of cooled cake.

Mrs. Frances Low
Westport, Indiana
September 1, 1970

Cranberry Coffeecake

This is perfect for the holidays.

- ¾ **cup margarine, softened**
- 1½ **cups granulated sugar**
- 3 **eggs, room temperature**
- 1½ **tsps. almond extract**
- 3 **cups all-purpose flour**
- 1½ **tsps. baking powder**
- 1½ **tsps. baking soda**
- ¾ **tsp. salt**
- 1½ **cups sour cream**
- 1 **16-oz. can whole-berry cranberry sauce**
- ½ **cup chopped nuts**

Glaze:
- ¾ **cup powdered sugar**
- 1 **Tbsp. warm water**
- ½ **tsp. almond extract**

In a large bowl, cream margarine and granulated sugar until light. Add eggs, 1 at a time, beating thoroughly after each addition. Beat in almond extract.

Sift together flour, baking powder, baking soda and salt. Add to creamed mixture alternately with sour cream, beating well after each addition. Spoon ⅓ of batter into greased and floured Bundt or other 12-cup tube pan. Distribute ⅓ of cranberry sauce over batter. Repeat layers 2 more times, ending with cranberry sauce. Sprinkle nuts over top. Bake at 350° for 1 hour or until cake tests done. Cool in pan 5 minutes. Remove from pan and cool on wire rack. Serve warm or cooled. Drizzle glaze over top. Makes 20 servings.

To make glaze, blend powdered sugar, extract and water in small bowl until smooth.

Trenda Leigh
Richmond, Virginia
December 19, 1989

Grandma West's Chocolate Cake

1 cup lard OR shortening
2 cups granulated sugar
2 beaten eggs
1 cup sour milk
½ cup cocoa
2½ cups flour
2 tsps. baking soda
½ tsp. salt
1 cup boiling water
1 tsp. vanilla

Beat together shortening, granulated sugar and eggs. Sour fresh milk with a few teaspoons of vinegar. Set aside. Sift cocoa, flour, soda and salt together. Add dry ingredients alternately with milk to the shortening mixture. Mix well. Add, last of all, boiling water and vanilla. Bake at 350° in greased and floured cake pans for about 20-25 minutes. It stays very moist if you don't overbake.

Lynn Lauterbach
Loveland, Colorado
September 11, 1990

Cherry Cheesecake

I'm a 17-year-old high school senior. I make this for family gatherings and it is very popular.

20 graham crackers, finely crushed
¼ cup melted margarine
¼ cup powdered sugar
1 8-oz. pkg. cream cheese
1 cup powdered sugar
1 tsp. vanilla
2 cups miniature marshmallows
1 can cherry pie filling
• whipped topping

Mix graham crackers, margarine and ¼ cup powdered sugar together. Press into 9x13-inch baking dish or pan. Chill.

Soften cream cheese to room temperature and mix together with the 1 cup powdered sugar, vanilla and marshmallows. Spread over chilled crust. Spread pie filling over top and chill. Serve with whipped topping. Keep refrigerated.

Mark Lamb
Hutchinson, Kansas
August 29, 1989

Best Rhubarb Shortcake

This is the best rhubarb recipe I've ever made in my 38 years of married life!

4   cups rhubarb
¾   cup granulated sugar
3   Tbsps. margarine OR butter
1   cup flour
1   tsp. baking powder
¼   tsp. salt
½   cup milk
1   cup granulated sugar
1   Tbsp. cornstarch
¼   tsp. salt
1   cup boiling water with few drops red food coloring

Place cubed or crushed rhubarb in 8x8-inch pan. Cream granulated sugar and margarine. Mix flour, baking powder and salt. Add milk and flour mixture to creamed mixture. Spread over rhubarb. Combine 1 cup granulated sugar, 1 tablespoon cornstarch and ¼ teaspoon salt. Sprinkle over top. Pour 1 cup boiling water over top. Bake in 350° oven for 1 hour. Serves 6-8.

Marilyn Keenan
Grinnell, Iowa
May 8, 1990

Baby Food Cake

This is such a delicious cake any time of the year. It's very moist and good on picnics or church dinners.

3   eggs
2   cups granulated sugar
1¼   cups salad oil
3   jars baby food: 1 applesauce, apricot and carrot
2   cups flour
2   tsps. cinnamon
2   tsps. baking soda
1   cup chopped pecans

Frosting:
½   cup margarine
1   8-oz. pkg. cream cheese
1   1-lb. box powdered sugar
1   tsp. vanilla

Combine eggs, granulated sugar and salad oil. Add baby food. Sift flour, cinnamon and baking soda and add to baby food mixture. Stir in pecans. Bake in 9x13x2-inch baking pan at 350° for 35 minutes.

For frosting, combine margarine, cream cheese, powdered sugar and vanilla. Frost cake when cool.

Vera Kaser
Omaha, Nebraska
July 7, 1992

Prince of Wales Cake

Cake:
- 1 cup brown sugar
- ½ cup margarine
- 3 egg yolks
- 2½ cups flour
- 1 tsp. baking soda
- 1 tsp. nutmeg
- 1 tsp. cloves
- 1 tsp. cinnamon
- 1 cup sour milk
- ½ lb. raisins, chopped

Icing:
- 1 cup granulated sugar
- 2 Tbsps. water
- 3 egg whites
- ½ lb. raisins

Cream brown sugar and margarine. Add egg yolks, 1 at a time, beating well after each addition. Sift dry ingredients together and add to creamed mixture alternately with sour milk and the chopped raisins, beginning and ending with dry mixture. Pour into two 8-inch, greased and floured pans. Bake at 325° for about 35 minutes.

To make icing: Boil granulated sugar and water until a thread forms. Beat egg whites until stiff. Continue beating, gradually adding the hot syrup. When stiff enough to spread, fold in raisins and ice the cake.

Dorothy Holifield
Irondale, Missouri
January 15, 1991

Unusual Frozen Cake

This is one you'll have to try.

- 1 regular size box white cake, mixed with milk instead of water
- • oil and eggs as per cake box directions
- 1 tsp. vanilla
- 1 cup chopped nuts
- 1 cup brown sugar
- ¼ cup cocoa
- 1¾ cups boiling water
- ½ tsp. burnt sugar flavoring OR vanilla
- • whipped topping

Add milk (instead of water) to cake mix, using the same amount as box instructs for water. Include oil and eggs according to box directions. Add vanilla and chopped nuts. Grease and flour a 9x13-inch pan. Pour batter into pan. Do not bake. Cover pan with foil or tight-fitting lid and freeze overnight.

The next day, combine brown sugar, cocoa, boiling water and burnt sugar flavoring or vanilla. Stir well. Preheat oven to 350°. Take cake from freezer, remove foil and pour cocoa mixture over frozen cake. Immediately bake for 1 hour or until done. Cool. Refrigerate if you like. Cut into squares. Remove squares with cake server and place upside down on plate. Top with whipped topping.

Dorothy Hiltgen
Waterville, Kansas
September 15, 1987

Poppy Seed Cake

This is a good recipe given to me by a friend years ago.

Cake:
- ½ cup poppy seeds
- 1 cup milk
- 1½ cups granulated sugar
- ½ cup shortening
- 1 egg
- 2 egg whites
- 1 tsp. vanilla
- 2 cups all-purpose flour, sifted twice
- 2 tsps. baking powder
- ½ tsp. salt

Filling:
- 1 egg yolk
- ½ cup milk
- ½ cup granulated sugar
- 1 tsp. cornstarch
- ½ tsp. vanilla
- ½ cup chopped pecans

Frosting:
- 2 egg whites
- ¾ cup granulated sugar
- ¼ cup water
- • dash of salt

For cake: Soak poppy seeds in milk overnight. Cream together granulated sugar and shortening. Add egg and egg whites, poppy seeds and milk mixture, vanilla, flour, baking powder and salt. Line two 8-inch cake pans with waxed paper. Pour batter into pans. Bake at 350° for 40 minutes or less. (Check frequently near end of baking time.)

For filling: Mix egg yolk, milk, granulated sugar and cornstarch in a small saucepan. Cook until it thickens, about 5 minutes. Add vanilla and pecans. Let cool. Spread mixture between cooled cake layers.

For frosting: Beat egg whites until they stand in peaks. Combine granulated sugar, water and salt; cook until mixture spins a small thread. Pour over the beaten egg whites. Beat until mixture stands in peaks. Frost cake.

Juaneta Heckman
Ottawa, Kansas
December 6, 1994

WHEN TIME IS SHORT
For a quick and easy dessert: Slice a store-bought pound cake or sponge cake into horizontal layers. Spread layers with preserves or jam. Put cake back together again. Slice and serve.

■ **BLEND THE FLAVOR**
To evenly distribute spices and flavorings in a batter, cream them with the fat.

Mexican Chocolate Chiffon Cake

This is so good!

¾ cup hot coffee
⅓ cup cocoa
1¾ cups sifted flour
1⅔ cups granulated sugar
½ tsp. salt
1½ tsps. soda
½ cup pure vegetable oil
7 egg yolks
2 tsps. vanilla
7 egg whites
½ tsp. cream of tartar

Blend hot coffee and cocoa and let cool. Sift flour, granulated sugar, salt and soda into a large bowl and make a well in the center. Add oil, egg yolks, vanilla and coffee mixture, beating until smooth. Beat egg whites and cream of tartar in a bowl until very stiff. Gradually pour chocolate mixture over egg whites, gently folding in until blended. Pour into 10-inch tube cake pan (we use an angel food cake pan) and bake in 325° oven for 55 minutes, then increase heat to 350° and continue baking 10-15 minutes longer.

Joe O. Gingerich
Hazleton, Iowa
July 7, 1987

Blueberry Surprise Cake

This cake is really a surprise because the berries sink to the bottom and the marshmallows rise to the top, forming a crust.

2 cups miniature marshmallows
2 cups fresh blueberries
1 3-oz. pkg. mixed-berry flavored gelatin
2½ cups flour
1 cup granulated sugar
½ cup shortening
3 tsps. baking powder
½ tsp. salt
1 cup milk
1 tsp. vanilla
3 eggs

Grease a 9x13-inch baking pan. Space marshmallows evenly across the bottom. Combine blueberries and their juice with the dry gelatin in a separate bowl; set aside. Combine remaining ingredients; beat well. Pour batter over marshmallows in pan and spoon berry-gelatin over the top of batter. Bake in a 350° oven for 30 minutes, then reduce heat to 300° and continue baking 15 minutes more. Marshmallows will rise to the top. Makes 12-15 servings.

Christine Gibson
Fontana, Wisconsin
May 7, 1991

Snow Mountain Cake

4   eggs
1   cup granulated sugar
½   cup sifted flour
¼   tsp. salt
1   tsp. baking powder
2   tsps. vanilla
1   cup dates
1   cup nuts, chopped
5   oranges
3   bananas
¼   cup granulated sugar
1   pint whipping cream
•   coconut

Beat eggs, add 1 cup granulated sugar, flour, salt and baking powder. Stir in vanilla, dates and nuts. Spread in two 8-inch oiled pans. Bake in 350° oven for 30 minutes. Cool.

Peel oranges, cut into bite-size pieces and add sliced bananas and ¼ cup granulated sugar. The sugar will make fruit juicy.

Tear cake into pieces. Make 1 round of cake pieces, 12 inches in diameter, in center of plate. Add some fruit, including some of the juice, to form another layer. Then add another layer of cake pieces until both fruit and cake are used. Punch and poke cake to form a mountain shape. Whip cream, adding 2-4 tablespoons granulated sugar, and frost "mountain." Sprinkle with coconut. Refrigerate cake for several hours. Serve with large spoon.

Edna Mae Fuller
Des Moines, Iowa
December 18, 1990

■ Potluck ■

*It doesn't shine like copper,
isn't light as aluminum.
It's black as coal and heavy,
almost seems to weigh a ton.*

*The outside's caked and rimy
while salt with bacon drippings
and a brown paper scrub
keeps the inside smooth and shiny.*

*Breakfast, dinner, supper,
continuously in use,
it shows no sign of wear,
seems impervious to abuse.*

*You can have your stainless steel.
Space-age Teflon just won't do.
That old iron skillet
is proven, tried and true.*

— J. Potter

Vanilla Wafer Cake

This is so good!

1	cup granulated sugar
6	eggs, separated
4½	cups crushed vanilla wafers
½	tsp. baking powder
1	cup milk
1	cup chopped nuts
1	cup coconut

Blend well: granulated sugar, egg yolks, vanilla wafer crumbs, baking powder, milk, nuts and coconut. Beat the egg whites stiffly, then fold into the above mixture. Bake in greased and floured tube pan at 350° for approximately 1 hour or until toothpick inserted in center comes out clean. Leave in inverted pan to cool. Makes 10-12 servings.

Mrs. C. Gibson
Fontana, Wisconsin
February 13, 1990

Skillet Apple Cake

This is a recipe that I just love. It is simple, dirties almost no dishes and can be altered to fit a diabetic diet. Best of all, it is very good!

1½	cups white flour
1	tsp. baking powder
½	tsp. salt
¼	tsp. nutmeg
½	tsp. cinnamon
½	tsp. ground cloves
1	cup granulated sugar
¾	cup salad oil
1	beaten egg
½	cup pecans OR other nuts
2	large apples, peeled and chopped

Sift flour, baking powder, salt, nutmeg, cinnamon, cloves and granulated sugar into iron skillet. Combine salad oil and egg. Add nuts and apples. Stir all together with dry ingredients and bake in 375° oven for 35 minutes.

Geneva Fairbanks
Rossville, Kansas
February 27, 1990

Caramel Pecan Cheesecake

1 cup graham cracker crumbs
¾ cup ground pecans
¼ cup granulated sugar
¼ cup butter, melted
12 ozs. cream cheese, softened
½ cup caramel ice cream topping
3 eggs
2 Tbsps. milk
½ cup dairy sour cream
¼ cup caramel topping
• pecan halves

In a mixing bowl, combine crumbs, ground pecans, granulated sugar and melted butter. Pat onto bottom and 1½ inches up sides of an 8-inch spring-form pan.

In a large mixer bowl, beat cream cheese until fluffy. Gradually beat in the ½ cup caramel topping. Add eggs and milk; beat just until blended.

Turn mixture into crust. Bake in 350° oven for 40-45 minutes until center is set. Cool in pan 15 minutes.

Combine sour cream and remaining caramel topping; spoon over cheesecake. Loosen sides of cheesecake from pan with spatula. Cool 30 minutes more; remove sides of pan. Cool. Chill. Garnish with pecan halves before serving. Makes 10-12 servings.

Joan Dixon
Westmont, Illinois
August 17, 1993

Sock-it-to-me Cake

This is one of our favorite cakes!

1 pkg. butter cake mix
½ cup granulated sugar
¾ cup oil
4 eggs
½ cup chopped nuts
½ pt. (1 cup) butter-milk
½ tsp. butter flavoring
2 Tbsps. brown sugar
2 tsps. cinnamon
1 cup powdered sugar
2 Tbsps. milk
½ tsp. vanilla
½ tsp. butter flavoring

Combine cake mix, granulated sugar and oil, mixing well. Add eggs, beating after each; add nuts, buttermilk and butter flavoring. Pour half of batter into a well-greased tube pan. Combine brown sugar and cinnamon and sprinkle on batter. Add remaining batter and bake 1 hour in 350° oven. Combine powdered sugar, milk, vanilla and butter flavoring. Drizzle over warm cake.

Ruth M. Colley
Kansas City, Missouri
September 2, 1986

Black Forest Cake

Here is a delicious cake for the summer months. It's easy!

- 1   18¼-oz. chocolate cake mix
- ¾   tsp. cinnamon
- 16 ozs. cherry yogurt
- 3   eggs
- ¼   cup milk
- 1   tsp. vanilla extract

Topping:
- 1   8-oz. carton frozen non-dairy whipped topping, thawed
- 1   21-oz. can cherry pie filling, chilled

Preheat oven to 350°. Line two 9-inch round cake pans with waxed paper, cut to fit; oil and flour sides of pan. In large mixing bowl, combine cake mix, cinnamon, yogurt, eggs, milk and vanilla. Mix at medium speed for 3 minutes until smooth. Turn batter evenly into prepared cake pans. Bake at 350° for 30-33 minutes, until toothpick inserted in center comes out clean. Cool on wire rack 15 minutes. Remove from pans, remove waxed paper and cool completely. To decorate, place 1 layer upside-down on a large platter. With cake decorator tube or spoon, circle edge of cake layer with 1 cup whipped topping. Spread 1 cup cherry pie filling within center. Spread 1 cup whipped topping over filling. Top with second cake layer. Tube or spoon remaining whipped topping around outer edge. Spread center with remaining cherry filling. Chill at least 1 hour before serving. Keep leftovers covered in refrigerator.

Flo Burtnett
Gage, Oklahoma
June 21, 1994

Orange Dessert Cake

1   box orange cake mix
1   large box of orange gelatin OR 2 small boxes
2   cups boiling water
7   ozs. lemon-lime soda
1   small pkg. instant vanilla pudding
1½ cups milk
1   pt. container whipped topping

Bake cake in a 9x13x2-inch cake pan. Mix orange gelatin with boiling water; add lemon-lime soda. When cake is done, poke holes in top with fork and pour gelatin evenly over cake. Refrigerate. When cake is cool, mix instant pudding according to package directions. When almost thick, fold in whipped topping. Spread over cake and refrigerate.

Dorothy Climer
Nora Springs, Iowa
July 21, 1992

Cold Oven Pound Cake

This cake is so good!

1½ cups (3 sticks) butter
1   8-oz. pkg. cream cheese
3   cups granulated sugar
6   eggs
3   cups flour
1   tsp. vanilla extract
1   tsp. lemon extract

Cream butter and cream cheese and add granulated sugar. Add eggs, 1 at a time, beating after each addition. Add flour and extracts. Pour into greased and floured tube pan. Put cake in cold oven and bake at 300° for 1½ hours or until done.

Mrs. P.B. Brothers
Richmond, Virginia
March 16, 1982

TOASTING NUTS

Toast nuts by spreading them in an even layer in a shallow baking pan. Place in 325° oven; toast for 5-10 minutes, stirring occasionally, just until lightly browned. Remove from pan and cool completely.

■ CAKE FIT FOR ROYALTY

The French have a tradition of baking a little ceramic figurine into a cake. The person who discovers the figurine in their slice of cake is "King" or "Queen" for the day.

Pumpkin Pie Cake

1 box yellow cake mix
1 egg
½ stick margarine, melted
3½ cups canned pumpkin
½ cup granulated sugar
2 tsps. cinnamon
⅔ cup canned milk
3 eggs

Topping:
1 cup cake mix
¼ stick margarine
¾ cup granulated sugar
• nutmeats (optional)

Reserve 1 cup cake mix for topping. To remainder add 1 egg and margarine. Press mixture into 9x13-inch pan. In another bowl, add canned pumpkin, granulated sugar, cinnamon, canned milk and 3 eggs, mixing well. Pour gently over pressed cake mix.

To reserve 1 cup cake mix, add ¼ stick margarine and ¾ cup granulated sugar for topping. (Add nutmeats if desired.) Sprinkle topping over pumpkin mixture. Bake in 350° oven for 55 minutes.

Rosalie Bloom
Rockton, Pennsylvania
November 7, 1989

Rich and Delicious Cake

This cake is very rich and is made of fine quality ingredients. Sometimes it is named after a well-known Dallas department store. It is good to take to church, family gatherings, dinners and picnics. It can be eaten as a finger food, too.

1 18.25-oz. yellow cake mix
¼ cup cooking oil
2 eggs
½ cup chopped nuts
1 8-oz. pkg. cream cheese, softened
4¼ cups powdered sugar
2 eggs, beaten
½ cup chopped nuts

Mix cake mix, oil, eggs, and ½ cup nuts by hand; pat into ungreased 9x12-inch cake pan. Mix cream cheese, powdered sugar, beaten eggs and other ½ cup nuts to make topping. Mix well and sprinkle over cake batter. Bake in 300° oven for 1 hour and 15 minutes.

Flo Burtnett
Gage, Oklahoma
December 5, 1989

■ Birthdays ■

Red devil's food cake
meant
somebody's birthday.
I requested
Mama's chicken 'n' dumplings
also
on mine.

No presents
graced our party
the money wasn't there, but
Mama's homemade
hand-mixed cake (with love) —
better than a present
anywhere.

Besides,
we only knew
the date called
birthday.
We never even suspected
(until we were older)
presents were part
of the fare.

— Bobbie McGrane

Desserts That Please

■ Desserts That Please ■

Fruit Pizza 139
Velvety Lime Squares 139
Spicy Pumpkin Bars with Cream Cheese Icing 140
Blackberry Cobbler 141
Caramel Apples 141
Dessert in a Pumpkin 142
Dried Apricot Cranberry Tart 142
Potica 143
Layered Rhubarb Dessert 144
Brazilian Custard 144
Cranberry Apple Crunch 145
Toasted Coconut Cream Dessert 145
Pumpkin Torte 146
Frozen Yogurt 147
Lemon Delight 147
Strawberry Mousse 148
Cranberry Pudding with Butter Sauce 148
Strawberry Fool 149
Custard's Last Stand 150
Cottage Cheese Delight 150
Sinfully Rich Dessert 151
Cranberry Potato Puffs 151
Strawberry Swirl 152
Cherry Angel Dessert 152
Earthquake Dessert 153
Peach Dumplings 153

Fruit Pizza

This fruit pizza really went like crazy at our church's salad luncheon.

Dough:
- 1½ cups flour
- ¾ cup margarine
- ½ cup powdered sugar

Filling:
- 1 8-oz. pkg. cream cheese
- ½ cup powdered sugar
- 2 tsps. vanilla

Fruit:
- peaches
- pears
- bananas (dip in lemon juice)
- strawberries
- apricots

Glaze:
- 1 cup pineapple juice
- ½ cup granulated sugar
- 2 tsps. cornstarch

Combine flour, margarine, powdered sugar and blend as for pie dough. Pat into an 11x14-inch pan. Bake in 325° oven for 20 minutes.

Mix together cream cheese, powdered sugar and vanilla. Spread on cooled crust.

Slice and arrange a selection of fruits over cheese mixture. Mix pineapple juice, granulated sugar and cornstarch in saucepan. Cook until thick. Pour over top of fruit.

Mary Kay Winter
Shell Rock, Iowa
July 3, 1990

Velvety Lime Squares

A pretty and refreshing spring dessert.

- 1 3-oz. can flaked coconut
- 2 cups vanilla wafer crumbs
- 2 Tbsps. butter, melted
- 2 Tbsps. granulated sugar
- 2 3-oz. pkgs. lime gelatin
- 2 cups boiling water
- 1 6-oz. can frozen limeade concentrate
- 3 pts. vanilla ice cream, softened
- ⅛ tsp. salt
- few drops green food coloring
- pecans for garnish, optional

Carefully toast ½ cup coconut in 375° oven until lightly browned, about 5 minutes. Set aside. Combine remaining coconut, vanilla wafer crumbs, butter and granulated sugar, and lightly press into a 7x11x1½-inch pan. Bake at 375° for 6-7 minutes. Cool. Dissolve gelatin in boiling water. Add limeade, ice cream, salt and food coloring, and stir until dissolved. Pour into baked crust. Top with reserved toasted coconut and garnish with pecans if you wish. Cover tightly and freeze until firm. Remove from freezer 20 minutes before cutting into squares.

Ann Klein
Osceola, Nebraska
May 24, 1994

Spicy Pumpkin Bars with Cream Cheese Icing

Bars:

2	cups flour
4	tsps. baking powder
1¼	tsps. cinnamon
1	tsp. nutmeg
1	tsp. ginger
½	tsp. salt
½	cup shortening
1	cup brown sugar
¼	cup granulated sugar
4	eggs
2	cups mashed pumpkin OR 1 16-oz. can pumpkin

Icing:

1	3-oz. pkg. cream cheese, softened
1	Tbsp. margarine
2½	cups powdered sugar
1	Tbsp. milk
1	tsp. vanilla

Grease a 10½x15½x1-inch jelly-roll pan. Heat oven to 350°. Sift together flour, baking powder, cinnamon, nutmeg, ginger and salt; set aside. Cream together shortening, brown sugar and granulated sugar in a bowl until light and fluffy. Add eggs 1 at a time, beating well after each addition. Beat in pumpkin. Gradually stir in dry ingredients, mixing well. Spread mixture in greased pan. Bake for 30 minutes or until top springs back when touched. Cool in pan on rack. For cream cheese icing, combine cream cheese, margarine, powdered sugar, milk and vanilla in a mixing bowl. Beat until smooth. Spread over bars and cut.

Rose M. Dietz
Hoisington, Kansas
October 25, 1994

COME FOR TEA

Entertaining takes on a new twist when the invitation reads "come for tea." This delightfully European custom lends itself to both intimate and grand celebrations, but whether it's for 2 or 22, no respectable tea can be without rich buttery cookies and other confections.

Taking tea, as the British refer to it, began in 1840 when Anna, the 7th Duchess of Bedford, requested that a tray laden with buttered bread, cake and tea be brought to her room to relieve the "sinking feeling" she experienced every afternoon around 4 o'clock. The idea soon spread to the Duchess' friends and became an elaborate ritual by the end of the century.

Today tea can be as simple or elaborate as you like. At the very least, however, the menu must include perfectly brewed tea with milk and lemon on the side, small finger sandwiches (or another savory) and a variety of breads, cakes, pastries and cookies.

Queen Victoria, known for her passion for sweets, can be credited with the custom of serving confections with tea.

Blackberry Cobbler

This is delicious served with cold milk or ice cream.

3   Tbsps. butter
1   cup granulated sugar
1   egg
1½   cups flour
½   tsp. salt
1   tsp. soda
½   tsp. cinnamon
½   tsp. cloves
2   Tbsps. vinegar
¼   cup blackberry juice OR milk
⅔   cup blackberries

Cream butter and granulated sugar. Add egg and beat until fluffy. Sift flour and measure. Sift all dry ingredients together and add alternately with juice and vinegar. Beat thoroughly after each addition.

Add berries and stir just enough to blend into dough. Pour into a greased 8-inch square pan and bake in 350° oven for approximately 40 minutes. Makes 6 servings.

Lorene Martin
Memphis, Missouri
August 18, 1987

Caramel Apples

Even dieters need to indulge occasionally—what better way than with apples covered with rich, homemade caramel?

1   cup (2 sticks) butter
2   cups firmly packed light brown sugar
1   cup light corn syrup
1   15-oz. can sweetened condensed milk
1   tsp. vanilla extract
8-10 wooden sticks
8-10 medium-sized apples

Melt butter in 3-quart heavy saucepan. Stir in brown sugar, corn syrup and condensed milk; mix well. Bring to boil over medium heat, stirring frequently. Cook to firm-ball stage (245°), stirring frequently, about 15-20 minutes. Remove from heat; stir in vanilla. Put a wooden stick in each apple at core. Dip apple into caramel mixture. Place on waxed paper to allow caramel to set. Store in cool, dry place at room temperature. Coats 8-10 apples.

Kate Marchbanks Food Story
October 25, 1994

Dessert in a Pumpkin

Cut off top of pumpkin and thoroughly clean out seeds and pulp. Fill center of pumpkin with mixture of apple slices, a few raisins, ½-1 cup of granulated sugar, 2 teaspoons cinnamon, 1 teaspoon nutmeg, a dash of ginger and cloves, and a few chopped nuts. Bake at 375° for about 1½ hours, or until apples and pumpkin meat are tender. Scoop out and serve topped with ice cream or half-and-half. Tastes like hot apple and pumpkin pie combined!

Starrlette L. Howard
Ogden, Utah
October 25, 1994

Dried Apricot Cranberry Tart

1 **packaged piecrust OR your own recipe**
⅓ **cup light brown sugar, packed**
⅓ **cup light corn syrup**
2 **eggs**
2 **Tbsps. melted butter OR margarine, cooled**
1 **tsp. vanilla**
¼ **tsp. salt**
¾ **cup dried apricots, chopped**
1 **cup fresh OR frozen cranberries**
½ **cup chopped walnuts**

Fit dough into 9-inch tart pan. Bake piecrust at 375° for 10-12 minutes or until golden; cool. Meanwhile, combine brown sugar and next 5 ingredients; whisk until smooth. Stir in dried apricots, cranberries and nuts. Pour into cooled piecrust and bake at 400° for 30 minutes. If desired, brush 24 dried apricot halves with corn syrup; arrange, overlapping, around edge of tart. Cool 10 minutes; serve with fresh whipped cream and garnish with mint sprig. Makes 6-8 servings.

Kate Marchbanks Food Story
February 27, 1990

Potica

This is an old Slavik recipe similar to a strudel.

Dough:
- 2 pkgs. active dry yeast
- ½ cup warm water
- 1 cup PLUS 4 Tbsps. buttermilk
- 2 eggs
- 1 stick butter OR margarine
- ½ cup granulated sugar
- 2½ tsps. baking powder
- 1 tsp. salt
- 6 cups flour OR more

Filling:
- 2 lbs. walnuts, finely ground
- 2 cups brown sugar
- 1 stick butter
- 2 eggs
- 1 tsp. vanilla
- 1 tsp. lemon extract
- ¼-½ cup milk OR more

In large mixing bowl, dissolve yeast in warm water. Add buttermilk, eggs, butter, granulated sugar, baking powder, salt and 2 cups flour. Blend slowly with electric mixer for 3 minutes. Add remaining flour. Knead into soft dough. Divide into 3 parts. Roll out on floured cloth, very thin.

Combine filling ingredients, mixing to a spreading consistency. Spread nut filling on each piece of rolled dough. Roll up dough by lifting cloth. Place in greased and floured bread pan. Let rise for 1 hour. Bake in 325-350° oven for 1 hour or until done. Makes 3 rolls.

Mrs. Harriet Bien
Rome, New York
January 30, 1990

■ A Culinary Caution ■

Beware of cooks. However kind
in face and mien, they are inclined
to violence in the extreme:
to scalding milk and whipping cream,
pickling things in briny kegs,
chopping nuts and beating eggs,
shredding the hapless lettuce leaf,
boiling rice and roasting beef;
all of which they learn from books
by master chefs. Beware of cooks.

— R.H. Grenville

Layered Rhubarb Dessert

A different way to fix rhubarb.

4   cups rhubarb,
    diced
1   cup granulated
    sugar
1   3-oz. box strawberry
    gelatin
½   box (2 cups) white
    OR yellow cake mix
⅓   cup melted butter,
    (drizzled on top)
1   cup water

Layer first 5 ingredients in 9x13-inch pan in order given. Pour water over all. Bake at 350° for 1 hour.

Winifred Jones
Sigourney, Iowa
July 5, 1994

Brazilian Custard

As much a national dish there as our apple pie is here. Yum! Melts in your mouth and is not watery, but creamier than American custards.

1   can condensed
    sweetened milk
1   can, refilled with
    regular milk
2-4 eggs (as you like)
1   tsp. vanilla
½   tsp. almond
    flavoring
½   cup maple syrup
½   cup coconut

Put condensed milk, regular milk, eggs, vanilla and almond flavoring in a blender and mix well.

In an ungreased casserole dish, 8x8-inches square (or similar medium-size round dish), put the mixed maple syrup and coconut. Pour the blended milk and egg ingredients over mixture.

Place dish in a larger pan of water to get a double-boiler effect and bake at 325° for 1 hour, until firm. Cool a bit, loosen sides with a table knife and invert on serving plate.

The coconut and syrup, which rise to the top while baking, will now be on the bottom of the dessert.

Serve plain or with whipped cream, sliced canned peaches or fresh strawberries.

Gloria Williams
Grandview, Missouri
May 10, 1994

Cranberry Apple Crunch

This makes a good fall dessert.

1 cup granulated sugar
1 cup water
2 cups cranberries
2 cups apples, peeled and chopped
1 cup rolled oats
½ cup brown sugar
⅓ cup flour
½ tsp. salt
¼ cup butter OR margarine
½ cup walnuts, broken

Mix granulated sugar and water; boil 5 minutes. Add cranberries and cook until skins pop, about 5 more minutes. Remove from heat. Add apples and pour into buttered 6x10x1½-inch baking dish. Mix oats, brown sugar, flour, salt and butter. Add broken walnuts. Sprinkle over top of fruit. Bake in moderate 350° oven for about 35 minutes. Cut into squares and serve warm with whipped cream.

Mrs. H.W. Walker
Richmond, Virginia
October 11, 1988

Toasted Coconut Cream Dessert

This is a quick-and-easy dessert.

1 cup flour
¼ cup brown sugar
½ cup margarine
1 cup coconut
2 boxes vanilla pudding mix
1 cup whipped topping

Mix flour, brown sugar, margarine and coconut. Spread on a cookie sheet and bake in 375° oven until brown, stirring occasionally.

Prepare the 2 boxes of pudding mix (or make your own pudding recipe) and let cool. Add whipped topping.

Put ¾ of the coconut mixture in a 9x9-inch pan. Add pudding. Sprinkle on remaining coconut mixture. Refrigerate.

Betty Ann Stutzman
Keota, Iowa
September 25, 1990

Pumpkin Torte

This is a little extra work, but well worth the effort.

Crust:
- 24 graham crackers, crushed
- ⅓ cup granulated sugar
- ½ cup butter

Filling:
- 1 8-oz. pkg. cream cheese
- 2 eggs, beaten
- ¾ cup granulated sugar
- 2 cups canned pumpkin
- 3 egg yolks
- ½ tsp. salt
- 1 tsp. cinnamon
- ½ cup milk
- 1 envelope unflavored gelatin
- ¼ cup cold water

Frosting:
- 3 egg whites
- ¼ cup granulated sugar
- 2 cups whipped topping

Mix cracker crumbs, granulated sugar and butter for crust. Press into a 9x12-inch pan, reserving ¼ cup for topping.

For filling, cream together cream cheese, eggs and granulated sugar. Place mixture on crust and bake for 20 minutes at 350°. Cook pumpkin, egg yolks, salt, cinnamon and milk until thick. Remove from heat and add gelatin dissolved in cold water. Cool. Spread on top of cream cheese mixture in crust. For frosting, beat egg whites and granulated sugar until peaks form. Fold in whipped topping. Spread over torte. Sprinkle reserved crumbs on top. Refrigerate. Makes 12-20 servings.

Mae Salzman
Kankakee, Illinois
November 8, 1994

■ Diet Dilemma ■

Skim milk is on my menu
Of fats, I am alert
I skip dips and rich dressings
But always have dessert.

— Helen Svaren

Frozen Yogurt

Orange flavored powdered soft drink mix and plain yogurt may be substituted for the strawberry.

- 3 8-oz. cups strawberry yogurt
- 1 envelope unsweetened strawberry flavored powdered drink mix
- 1 cup granulated sugar
- 2 cups whipped topping

Mix yogurt, drink mix and granulated sugar in a large bowl. Set in freezer until partially frozen, about 30 minutes. Remove from freezer and beat for about 5 minutes. Add whipped topping and beat until completely blended. Pour into half-gallon container and freeze.

Mrs. Eva Simpson
Dixon, Illinois
July 31, 1990

Lemon Delight

Such a refreshing dessert!

- 1½ sticks margarine
- 1½ cups flour
- ⅔ cup chopped pecans
- 1 8-oz. pkg. cream cheese
- 1 cup powdered sugar
- 1 8-oz. carton whipped topping
- 3 cups milk
- 2 pkgs. lemon instant pudding mix

Cream margarine and flour; add pecans. Pat mixture into bottom of 9x13-inch pan. Bake in 350° oven for 30 minutes. Mix cream cheese with powdered sugar and add half of the whipped topping. Spread on the crust. Beat milk, 1 cup at a time, with instant pudding mix and pour over cheese mixture. Top this with remaining whipped topping and refrigerate overnight. Cut into squares to serve 12.

Ruth McGurk
Huron, Ohio
March 29, 1988

Strawberry Mousse

1 lb. thawed frozen strawberries
¼ cup granulated sugar
• juice from ½ lemon
1 cup sour cream
½ cup milk
1 tsp. vanilla extract

Purée strawberries with granulated sugar and lemon juice. Mix sour cream, vanilla and milk with electric beater. Stir in strawberries. Pour contents into a bowl and freeze for 3 hours. Spoon into dessert cups and serve.

Mrs. L.W. Mayer
Richmond, Virginia
May 7, 1991

Cranberry Pudding with Butter Sauce

This is so good!

1½ cups flour
¾ cup granulated sugar
1 Tbsp. baking powder
3 Tbsps. butter, melted and cooled
1½ cups (6 ozs.) fresh cranberries, coarsely chopped
⅔ cup milk

Butter Sauce:
½ cup butter
2 cups granulated sugar
¾ cup half-and-half

Sift together flour, granulated sugar and baking powder into mixing bowl. Make a well in center and add butter, cranberries and milk. Stir until just moistened. Turn into buttered 1-quart casserole dish. Bake 55 minutes in 350° oven. Serve warm with butter sauce.

To make butter sauce, melt butter in top of double boiler. Gradually add the granulated sugar, stirring until dissolved. Gently stir in the half-and-half. This takes about 15 minutes.

Beth Marriott
Grinnell, Kansas
January 7, 1992

Strawberry Fool

Save a few berries for garnish to decorate the topping. A sprig of fresh mint leaves add to this pretty dessert.

- 2 **cups frozen OR fresh strawberries**
- ¼ **cup granulated sugar**
- 4 **whole eggs, lightly beaten**
- ½ **cup granulated sugar**
- ¼ **tsp. salt**
- 2½ **cups milk, carefully scalded**
- 1½ **tsps. vanilla extract**

Chantilly Cream:
- 1 **cup whipping cream**
- 4 **heaping Tbsps. powdered sugar**
- 1 **tsp. vanilla extract**

Wash and clean 2 cups of fresh strawberries. Crush them to a pulp with a fork. Sprinkle them with granulated sugar to taste. Stir the purée to be sure all sugar is dissolved. Let stand at least 1 hour in refrigerator.

Combine beaten eggs with ½ cup granulated sugar and salt in top of double boiler. Slowly add the scalded milk to eggs, stirring. Make sure hot water in bottom of double boiler is not touching the bottom of the top pan. Stir constantly while it simmers. Cook until custard coats a metal spoon. Remove at once from the heat. Place pan over a large bowl filled with ice cubes so that it cools quickly. Stir in vanilla. Cover bowl tightly with plastic wrap or foil and chill several hours or overnight.

To make Chantilly Cream: In cold bowl, beat whipping cream with an electric mixer or by hand until it stands in peaks. Gradually add the powdered sugar and vanilla. Make sure it is thoroughly mixed.

To make a pretty serving, layer the strawberry purée and custard into parfait glasses, making 2-3 layers. Or, to have a marbled effect, fold them gently together. Garnish with Chantilly Cream, whole strawberries and mint leaves. Makes 4-6 servings.

Shirley Levi
San Clemente, California
June 18, 1991

Custard's Last Stand

1 cup cooked grits
1 cup cottage cheese
1 cup vanilla yogurt
2 eggs
½ cup honey
1 tsp. vanilla extract
½ tsp. salt
½ cup raisins

Topping:
¼ cup light brown sugar
½ cup flour
2 Tbsps. butter, softened

Preheat oven to 350°. In food processor or blender, combine cooked grits and cottage cheese; process until smooth. Add yogurt, eggs, honey, vanilla and salt. Process until creamy.

Place raisins in bottom of 1½-quart casserole dish. Pour custard mixture over raisins. Bake, uncovered, for 25 minutes. In a bowl, combine brown sugar, flour and butter, cutting in until mixture resembles coarse meal. Sprinkle on top of custard and return to oven. Bake 15 minutes longer. Makes 6 servings.

Trenda Leigh
Richmond, Virginia
August 18, 1992

Cottage Cheese Delight

I thought this recipe would be of interest to my Capper's friends. We had a chance to partake of this tasty dish when we had the pleasure of visiting the Babbling Brook Inn located in Santa Cruz, California.

1 lb. grated Monterey Jack cheese
1 cup milk
1 cup flour
1 pt. low-fat cottage cheese
6 eggs
½ cup melted butter
• bread crumbs

Grease an 8x8-inch or 9x9-inch pan and sprinkle with grated cheese. Combine milk, flour, cottage cheese, eggs and melted butter. Pour over cheese in pan. Top with buttered bread crumbs. Bake at 350° for 45 minutes. Cut into squares. Top with sour cream and fruit conserve or fresh fruit, if desired. Leftover squares may be warmed in the microwave for 1 minute.

Mrs. P. Hughley
New York, New York
July 4, 1989

Sinfully Rich Dessert

Great for club meetings.

2 boxes of chocolate mousse mix
1 12-oz. container whipped topping
1 box Jiffy brownie mix
2 Heath candy bars

Bake brownie mix according to box directions. Cool and break into pieces in a 9x13-inch pan. Mix mousse according to package directions. Alternate layers of mousse with whipped topping on top of brownies. Sprinkle broken Heath bars over top. Chill.

Aletha J. Hansen
Kimballton, Iowa
March 12, 1991

Cranberry Potato Puffs

1½ cups hot un-seasoned mashed potatoes
⅓ cup melted butter
2 cups granulated sugar
3 eggs
1 cup buttermilk
1 tsp. vanilla
5½ cups sifted flour
4 tsps. baking powder
1½ tsps. baking soda
1 tsp. salt
½ cup chopped cranberries

Beat together the potatoes, butter, granulated sugar, eggs, buttermilk and vanilla until well blended. Sift together and stir in the flour, baking powder, baking soda and salt. Fold in the chopped cranberries. Chill for 1 hour. Drop rounded teaspoonfuls of dough into hot (360°) oil. Brown on both sides and drain on paper towels. Roll in granulated sugar before serving. Makes about 6 dozen.

Joan Dixon
Westmont, Illinois
December 22, 1992

COCONUT SERVING TIPS

Versatile coconut can be enjoyed in a variety of ways:
■ Toss with fruit for light desserts.
■ Add coconut to salads—fruit salads, chicken or tuna salads, carrot-raisin salads.
■ Toast coconut like this: Spread in a shallow pan, then toast at 350°, stirring often, until lightly browned, 7-10 minutes. Sprinkle on ice cream, cakes and salads.
■ Roll scoops of ice cream or sherbet in coconut; freeze to serve later.

Strawberry Swirl

1 cup graham cracker crumbs
1 Tbsp. granulated sugar
¼ cup butter, melted
2 cups sliced, fresh strawberries, OR 1 10-oz. pkg. frozen sliced strawberries, thawed
2 Tbsps. granulated sugar
1 3-oz. pkg. strawberry flavored gelatin
1 cup boiling water
½ lb. marshmallows
½ cup milk
1 cup whipping cream, whipped

Mix cracker crumbs, 1 tablespoon granulated sugar and butter. Press firmly over bottom of 9x9x2-inch baking pan. Chill until set. Sprinkle 2 tablespoons granulated sugar over fresh berries and let stand 30 minutes. Dissolve gelatin in boiling water. Drain berries, reserving the juice. Add water to juice to make 1 cup. Add to gelatin. Chill until partially set.

Meanwhile, combine marshmallows and milk in top of double boiler; stir until marshmallows melt. Cool thoroughly, then fold in whipped cream. Add strawberries to gelatin, then swirl in marshmallow mixture to give a marbled look. Pour into crust and chill until set.

Flo Burtnett
Gage, Oklahoma
May 9, 1989

Cherry Angel Dessert

Make this dessert the evening before for serving the next day. Pretty and delicious!

8 cups ½-inch cubes of angel food cake
1 No. 2 can cherry pie filling
1 pkg. instant vanilla pudding
1½ cups milk
1 cup dairy sour cream

Place half of cake pieces in 9x9x2-inch pan. Reserve ⅓ cup cherry pie filling and spread remainder over cake cubes in pan. Top with remaining cake cubes. Combine pudding mix, milk and sour cream, beating until smooth. Spoon over cake cube layer. Chill for 5 hours. Cut in squares and garnish with reserved cherry pie filling.

Adela Eret
Fairbury, Nebraska
March 19, 1968

Earthquake Dessert

This is unusual and very good.

- coconut, enough to cover pan bottom
- 1 cup chopped nuts
- 1 German chocolate cake mix
- 1 stick soft margarine
- 1 lb. powdered sugar
- 1 8-oz. pkg. cream cheese, room temperature

Grease a 9x13x3-inch pan. (If you use a 9x13x2-inch pan, you will have runover in your oven.) Cover bottom with coconut, as much as you desire. Cover coconut with chopped nuts.

Prepare cake mix as directed on package. Pour over coconut-nut mixture. Combine margarine, powdered sugar and cream cheese. Stir until smooth. Spoon over cake mix; do not stir. Bake in 350° oven for 1 hour.

Blanche M. Bright
Reedsport, Oregon
February 2, 1993

Peach Dumplings

Here's a quick dessert.

- 1 pkg. refrigerated crescent rolls
- ¼ cup brown sugar
- 1 Tbsp. flour
- ½ tsp. nutmeg
- 4 fresh peaches, peeled, halved and pitted
- 8 pecan halves
- milk
- brown OR granulated sugar

Divide crescent rolls into 4 portions (2 triangles to each portion) and roll into squares. Combine brown sugar, flour and nutmeg in a mixing bowl; blend thoroughly.

Roll peach halves in brown sugar mixture; place 2 pecan halves in center of cavity and sandwich 2 halves together to form a whole peach. Place each in center of a dough square and bring ends of dough up, pinching to seal. Brush with milk and sprinkle lightly with brown or granulated sugar. Repeat with remaining peaches and dough.

Place dough-wrapped peaches on cookie sheet and bake in 375° oven 12-15 minutes or until golden brown. May be served warm or at room temperature. Makes 4 servings.

Dorothy Bohling
Perry, Oklahoma
August 2, 1983

■ A Cook's Dilemma ■

I didn't have potatoes,
So I substituted rice.
I didn't have paprika,
So I used another spice.
I didn't have tomato sauce,
I used tomato paste,
A whole can, not a half;
I don't believe in waste.
A friend gave me the recipe;
She said you couldn't beat it.
There must be something wrong with her,
I couldn't even eat it.

— **Velma Phillips**

Pies
For All
Seasons

■ Pies For All Seasons ■

Apple-Orange Pie 157
Granny's Angel Food Pie 158
Gingered Pear-Topped Mincemeat Pie .158
Creamy Maple Praline Pie 159
Fruit Cocktail Parfait Pie 160
Chocolate Cream Pecan Pie 160
Chocolate Pie 161
Mincemeat Ice Cream Pie 161
Peanut Butter Pie 162
Wonderful Walnut Pie 162
Fresh Peach Pie 163
Zucchini Pie 163
Butter Pecan Apple Pie 164
Drumstick Ice Cream Pie 164
Strawberry-Pudding Pie 165
Rhubarb-and-Strawberry Pie 165
Watermelon Chiffon Pie 166
Danggood Pie 166
Topsy Turvy Apple Pecan Pie 167
Oatmeal Pie 168
White Christmas Pie 168
Banana Split Pie 169
German's Chocolate Pie 169
Apple Butter Pie 170
Sugarless Apple Pie 171
Caramel Pecan Pie 171

■ Fitness for All ■

*Our bread is no longer just flour
It's wheat germ and yogurt and bran,
To fortify cells in our bodies
According to nature's best plan.*

*So now as we stroll out each morning
To feed crusts to squirrels and birds
Those hungry sweet woodland creatures
Are growing too healthy for words!*

— Catherine Mary Weidum

Apple-Orange Pie

2 thin-skinned juice oranges, well scrubbed
1 cup water
¼ cup honey
1 Tbsp. lemon juice
• pastry for 9-inch double crust pie
½ cup packed brown sugar
3 Tbsps. flour
• generous ¼ tsp. ground cinnamon
⅛ tsp. ground ginger
• generous pinch salt
6 medium Golden Delicious apples, cored and sliced
1 beaten egg for glaze

Slice 1 orange as thinly as possible, discarding seeds.

Thinly pare and julienne cut the peel of remaining orange. Combine water, honey and lemon juice in a large saucepan. Bring to a boil. Add orange slices and peel. Cover, reduce heat and simmer until peel is limp and easily chewed, about 1½ hours. Drain orange, gently press out extra liquid and set aside.

In a bowl, combine brown sugar, flour, spices and salt. Add apple slices and toss until evenly coated. Place half of apple slices in a pastry-lined 9-inch pie plate, then the cooked orange and the remaining apple slices. Place top crust over filling. Crimp edges and slash top crust in a few places to allow steam to escape. Brush top with beaten egg.

Bake in preheated 350° oven for 1 hour.

Kate Marchbanks Food Story April 23, 1991

B ETTER PIE CRUSTS

■ For a sweetened crust, 1-3 Tbsps. of granulated sugar can be added to the flour and salt before the shortening is cut in.

■ For a cheese crust—delicious with apple pies as well as chicken pot pie or quiche—add ½ cup of grated cheese for each 1⅓ cups of flour.

■ For a spiced crust, add ½ tsp. cinnamon, nutmeg or apple pie spice to each cup of flour.

■ For an herbed crust, add ½ tsp. dried herbs or 1 Tbsp. chopped fresh herbs for each cup of flour.

■ PERFECT PIE CRUST EDGES

Shield the edges of the crust with foil before the end of the baking time or reduce oven temperature to keep edges from becoming too brown.

Granny's Angel Food Pie

I found this recipe and it is just like my grandmother's.

- 1 baked pie crust
- 2 cups boiling water
- 1¼ cups granulated sugar
- • pinch of salt
- 1 tsp. vanilla
- 2 heaping Tbsps. cornstarch
- 2 stiffly beaten egg whites
- • whipped cream OR topping
- • nutmeats

Mix dry ingredients and pour boiling water over them. Cook in double boiler until thick. Add vanilla; slowly fold mixture into stiffly beaten egg whites. Pour into baked pie crust and cool. Top with whipped cream and nutmeats.

Mrs. Hazel Wolf
Keosauqua, Iowa
June 23, 1992

Gingered Pear-Topped Mincemeat Pie

- 1 9-inch unbaked pastry shell
- 1 27-oz. jar ready-to-use mincemeat
- 2 medium pears, cored, pared and sliced
- 2½ tsps. finely chopped crystallized ginger

Place rack in lowest position in oven. Preheat oven to 400°. Reserve ¼ cup mincemeat. Spread remaining mincemeat in pastry shell.

In small bowl, combine pear slices and reserved mincemeat; mix well. Arrange pear slices on top of pie. Sprinkle ginger over pear slices. Bake 30 minutes. Reduce oven temperature to 325°. Bake 10 minutes longer. Cool. Garnish as desired. Store mincemeat pie covered at room temperature.

Kate Marchbanks Food Story
November 22, 1994

Creamy Maple Praline Pie

This pie makes "maple maniacs" out of just about everyone!

¼	**cup butter**
¼	**cup light brown sugar, firmly packed**
2	**cups pecans, finely chopped**
1	**envelope unflavored gelatin**
¼	**cup cold water**
1	**8-oz. pkg. cream cheese**
¾	**cup maple syrup**
1	**cup whipping cream, whipped**
•	**fresh mint sprigs**

Preheat oven to 350°. Cream butter with brown sugar. Mix in 1½ cups pecans. Press evenly into 9-inch ovenproof glass pie plate. Bake until edges begin to brown, about 15 minutes. Cool.

Sprinkle gelatin over water in small bowl. Let mixture stand 5 minutes to soften. Set bowl in pan of simmering water and stir until gelatin is completely dissolved.

Mix cream cheese in processor until smooth. With machine running, gradually pour syrup through feed tube and mix until smooth. Blend in dissolved gelatin. Transfer to large bowl. Fold in whipping cream and remaining pecans. Spoon into cooled crust. Cover and refrigerate until filling is set, at least 12 hours. Garnish with mint sprigs. Serve pie chilled.

Ryan Primiano
Maple Heights, Ohio
September 13, 1994

■ Pumpkin Pie Saga ■

Out of the oven and into plain sight;
I just might sneak a bite!
It smells spicy and very pleasant;
It even smells better than the fresh roasted pheasant.

My nostrils breathe the delicious smell in,
and I hear it bubbling over the din.
During the prayer....
Toward the pie my hand crept through the air.

But the pie was terribly hot,
Unfortunately I did not give that a thought.
So my hand got a burn,
And a lesson I did learn.
Never ever stick a finger into Granny's pumpkin pie!

— Jonathan Conard, Age 11

Fruit Cocktail Parfait Pie

Make this pie for an elegant treat. It is as pretty as it is delicious.

1   baked 9-inch pastry shell
1   17-oz. can fruit cocktail
¾   cup water
1   3-oz. pkg. lime gelatin
1   pt. vanilla ice cream
•   whipping cream

Drain fruit cocktail, reserving syrup. Pour syrup and water into a 2-quart saucepan. Bring to a boil, remove from heat. Add gelatin, stir until dissolved. Cut ice cream into 6-8 pieces. Blend into hot gelatin until melted. Chill until partly set. Fold in fruit, pour into pastry shell. Chill to set. Serve with whipped cream. Makes 8 servings.

E. Dotterman
Mastic, New York
April 18, 1978

Chocolate Cream Pecan Pie

This is a "convenience" pie.

2   squares unsweetened chocolate
2   Tbsps. butter OR margarine
2   Tbsps. hot milk
⅔   cup sifted powdered sugar
1½   cups toasted, shredded coconut
1   pkg. chocolate pie filling (not instant)
1   pkg. vanilla pie filling (not instant)
½   cup chopped pecans
½   pt. whipping cream

Melt and blend unsweetened chocolate and butter. Mix milk and powdered sugar and stir into chocolate mixture. Add and thoroughly mix coconut. Spread on surface of greased 9-inch pie pan. Chill until firm. Prepare vanilla and chocolate pie filling together, according to package directions. Remove from heat and add chopped nuts. Cool. Pour into chocolate pie crust. Top with whipped cream sweetened with 2 tablespoons granulated sugar.

Mrs. R.E. Becket
Los Angeles, California
January 7, 1969

Chocolate Pie

I'm always looking for new recipes. We especially like this since there are no eggs in it.

1   cup granulated sugar
5   heaping Tbsps. all-purpose flour
5   Tbsps. cocoa (level)
½   tsp. salt
2½ cups boiling water
2   tsps. vanilla
•   butter the size of a walnut

Mix granulated sugar, flour, cocoa and salt. Pour into boiling water and cook until thick. Add butter and vanilla. Stir until blended. Pour into baked pie shell.

Margaret Slater
Caldwell, Kansas
January 5, 1993

Mincemeat Ice Cream Pie

This is a terrific dessert.

1   sponge, angel OR pound cake loaf (10x4x2-inch)
1   qt. vanilla ice cream
1   cup prepared mincemeat
½   cup slivered, blanched almonds, toasted
1   tsp. grated orange peel
1   cup whipped topping
•   almonds
•   maraschino cherries

Rub brown crumbs off cake. Cut cake lengthwise in 3 even layers. Stir ice cream to soften. Fold in mincemeat, almonds and orange peel. Spread between cake layers. Freeze firm. Before serving frost top and sides with whipped topping. Trim with almonds and maraschino cherries. Makes about 10 servings.

Vivian M. Preston
Barberton, Ohio
November 21, 1989

Peanut Butter Pie

A county fair grand champion recipe. You'll take an empty pan home when you serve this pie!

Crust:
1¼ cups chocolate sandwich cookie crumbs
¼ cup granulated sugar
¼ cup butter OR margarine, melted

Filling:
1 cup creamy peanut butter
1 8-oz. pkg. cream cheese, softened
1 cup granulated sugar
1 Tbsp. margarine, softened
1 tsp. vanilla
1 cup heavy cream, whipped
• grated chocolate sandwich cookie crumbs, optional

Combine crust ingredients, press into a 9-inch pie plate. Bake at 375° for 10 minutes. Cool.

In a mixing bowl, beat peanut butter, cream cheese, granulated sugar, margarine and vanilla until smooth. Fold in whipped cream. Gently spoon into crust. Garnish with crumbs, if desired. Refrigerate. Makes 8-10 servings.

Miranda Pittenger
Cooperstown, North Dakota
May 10, 1994

Wonderful Walnut Pie

This pie is wonderful!

1 unbaked 9-inch pie shell
½ cup brown sugar, packed
½ cup soft butter
¾ cup granulated sugar
3 eggs
½ tsp. salt
¼ cup white corn syrup
½ cup light cream
1 cup broken walnut meats
½ tsp. vanilla
7 walnut halves

In top of double boiler, cream together brown sugar and butter. Stir in granulated sugar, eggs, salt, corn syrup and cream. Cook over hot, but not boiling, water for 5 minutes, stirring constantly. Remove from heat. Stir in broken nuts and vanilla. Pour into crust. Bake in 350° oven for 50 minutes. Arrange walnut halves around top of pie and bake 15 minutes longer. Cool on wire rack. Serve with ice cream or whipped cream or plain. (For toasty nuts on top, bake pie for 15 minutes, then arrange nuts on top and bake 50 minutes longer.)

Mrs. Orlin Petersen
Utica, South Dakota
January 3, 1989

Fresh Peach Pie

This is one of our summer-time favorites!

1 baked pie crust, cooled
1 8-oz. pkg. cream cheese
1 cup granulated sugar (or sugar substitute), divided
1 tsp. vanilla
1 small pkg. peach gelatin
6 large ripe peaches, peeled and sliced
2 Tbsps. lemon juice

Beat cream cheese until fluffy. Blend in ½ cup granulated sugar (or sugar substitute) and vanilla. Spread on bottom and sides of pie shell. Chill. (This may be done a day ahead.) Slice peaches into bowl, sprinkle with lemon juice and add the remaining ½ cup granulated sugar or sugar substitute. Stir and chill for 3 or 4 hours. Take peaches out and strain off accumulated juice, reserving liquid. Add water (if necessary) to make 1½ cups of liquid. Heat to boiling and add 1 package peach gelatin. Cool and then quick-chill in freezer until syrupy or almost set up. Add to peaches. Mix and pour into pie shell. Chill until set. Serve with whipped cream or ice cream.

Linda McAhren
Wichita, Kansas
August 30, 1994

Zucchini Pie

This tastes like Dutch apple pie.

4 cups zucchini*
1½ tsps. cream of tartar
• dash of salt
2 Tbsps. flour
1 Tbsp. lemon juice
• dash of nutmeg
1¼ cups granulated sugar
1½ tsps. cinnamon
1 tsp. butter (approximately)
1 9-inch unbaked pie shell

Topping:
1 stick margarine
½ cup granulated sugar
1 cup flour

*Peel zucchini. Cut lengthwise; scoop out seeds. Slice to resemble apple slices.

Cook zucchini 10 minutes in small amount of water. Drain. Mix cream of tartar, salt, flour, lemon juice, nutmeg, granulated sugar and cinnamon with zucchini. Pour into unbaked pie shell. Dot with butter.

Make topping by mixing margarine, granulated sugar and flour and crumbling over ingredients in pie shell. Bake at 375° for 45 minutes.

Ethel Kuhn
Ottumwa, Iowa
July 5, 1994

Butter Pecan Apple Pie

This pie is an original recipe. It won first prize in a local pie baking contest.

1   unbaked pie crust
6   tart apples
2   Tbsps. water
¾   cup granulated sugar
2½   Tbsps. cornstarch
⅛   tsp. salt
½   tsp. cinnamon
½   cup water
1   16-oz. can butter pecan frosting

Peel and thinly slice apples. Cook with 2 tablespoons water for 5 minutes. Remove from heat. Mix granulated sugar, cornstarch, salt and cinnamon. Stir in ½ cup water to make a thin paste. Stir into apples. Pour filling into pie crust. Bake at 400° for 10 minutes, then at 325° for 35 minutes. Top with frosting.

Evelyn Kennell
Roanoke, Illinois
March 12, 1991

Drumstick Ice Cream Pie

Now here's a just right dessert for summer.

•   graham crackers
¼   cup crunchy peanut butter
¼   cup melted margarine
2   tsps. granulated sugar
1   qt. vanilla ice cream
1   12-oz. pkg. chocolate chips
•   crushed peanuts

Crush enough graham crackers for a 9-inch pie crust. Add peanut butter, margarine and granulated sugar to crumbs. Place in 9-inch pie pan and bake in 350° oven for 8-10 minutes. Cool.

Press ice cream over crust in pan. Melt chocolate chips in double boiler. Cool slightly and pour over ice cream. Top with crushed peanuts. Put pie in freezer. To serve, remove from freezer 5-10 minutes before and cut into 8 pieces.

*Editor's Note: Using 12 ounces of chocolate chips will produce a thick topping that may make cutting difficult. For ease in serving, you may wish to reduce the amount of chocolate chips to 3 ounces, or substitute chocolate shavings.

Alice Hugo
Tulsa, Oklahoma
July 18, 1989

Strawberry-Pudding Pie

This strawberry pie is super quick to make, and delicious, too! You can use fresh or frozen berries, making it a year-round pie.

- 1 ready-to-use graham cracker crust OR your favorite graham crust
- 4 cups sliced strawberries, reserving a few for garnish (If using frozen berries, omit the following ½ cup granulated sugar)
- ½ cup granulated sugar
- 1 3½-oz. pkg. vanilla instant pudding, dry
- 1 8-oz. container whipped topping

Add granulated sugar to berries if using fresh. Add the dry pudding mix to whipped topping. Add strawberries and spoon into crust. Keep refrigerated and use within 2 days. Preparation time is about 5 minutes.

Waydella Hart
Bartlett, Kansas
May 21, 1991

Rhubarb-and-Strawberry Pie

This is our favorite pie recipe.

- 2 cups rhubarb, diced
- 2 cups strawberries
- 2 cups granulated sugar
- ¼ cup flour
- • dough for 2-crust pie
- • butter

Mix granulated sugar and flour. Add ¾ of mixture to fruits. Put remaining flour and granulated sugar mixture in unbaked pie shell. Add fruit. Dot with butter. Add top crust. Bake in 420° oven for 10 minutes. Reduce temperature to 350° and bake 35 minutes more.

Vada Harmon
Ordway, Colorado
July 16, 1991

Watermelon Chiffon Pie

A good summertime pie.

3½ lbs. ripe watermelon
⅓ cup granulated sugar
⅛ tsp. salt
1 envelope unflavored gelatin
2 tsps. lemon juice
2 egg whites
½ cup whipping cream
1 9-inch graham cracker crust

Cut watermelon into cubes, discarding rind and seeds. Process watermelon in blender or food processor until smooth. After straining and discarding pulp, you should have 1½ cups juice. Pour juice into saucepan and add granulated sugar and salt. Sprinkle gelatin over top, and let stand 5 minutes to soften. Stir over medium heat until gelatin is dissolved, then add lemon juice. Cover and refrigerate 1 hour or until mixture thickens and mounds slightly when dropped from spoon. Whip the egg whites and fold into gelatin mixture. Whip cream and fold all together. Spoon into pie shell. Chill 6-8 hours or overnight in refrigerator.

Ardes Bier
Clear Lake, Iowa
August 17, 1982

Danggood Pie

Recently I tried this recipe and found the pie to be excellent. I use Del Monte pineapple and do not drain it. There isn't much juice.

1½ cups granulated sugar
1 cup crushed pineapple, undrained
3 eggs, lightly beaten
3 Tbsps. all-purpose flour
1 cup coconut flakes
¾ stick butter OR margarine
1 unbaked 9-inch pie shell

Stir together the granulated sugar, pineapple, eggs, flour and coconut flakes. Melt butter and combine with other ingredients. Pour filling into unbaked pie shell. Bake for 60 minutes at 350° or until filling is set and browned.

Mrs. Madonna Jamison
Lindsborg, Kansas
March 16, 1982

Topsy Turvy Apple Pecan Pie

You'll flip over this dessert.

¼ **cup softened butter OR margarine**
½ **cup pecan halves**
⅔ **cup firmly packed brown sugar**
6 **cups sliced Jonathan apples (about 2½ lbs.)**
2 **Tbsps. lemon juice**
1 **Tbsp. flour**
½ **cup granulated sugar**
½ **tsp. cinnamon**
½ **tsp. nutmeg**
¼ **tsp. salt**
• **pastry for 2-crust pie**

Spread softened butter evenly on bottom and sides of 9-inch pie pan. Press pecan halves, rounded side down, into butter. Pat brown sugar evenly over pecans. Roll out enough pastry for 1 crust. Place in pie pan over granulated sugar; trim, leaving ½-inch overhang. Combine remaining ingredients. Pour into pie pan, keeping top level. Top with remaining pastry. Trim evenly with bottom crust and fold edges together flush with rim. Flute and prick top of pie with fork. Bake in hot oven (450°) for 10 minutes; reduce heat to moderate (350°) and bake 30-45 minutes longer, or until apples are tender. Remove from oven. When syrup in pan stops bubbling, place serving plate over pie and invert. Carefully remove pie pan. Serve hot.

Edna Drake
Perry, Missouri
October 5, 1976

■ Eating Out ■

Frankly, my dear, I do not care
To picnic in the open air
With insects in possessive mood
Whose fancy is to share my food.

Alfresco fare does not appeal
To one who craves a home-cooked meal,
Especially when there's every chance
Of eating charred beef laced with ants.

Let's keep the outdoors where it's at,
Fast food cafe for fly and gnat
While we dine the old-fashioned way
Indoors, in comfort. That's gourmet!

— D.L. Winkler

Oatmeal Pie

This pie tastes similar to a pecan pie, but is not as rich.

Filling:
- 3 eggs, well beaten
- ⅔ cup granulated sugar
- 1 cup brown sugar
- 2 Tbsps. butter
- ⅔ cup quick cooking oats
- ⅔ cup coconut
- 1 tsp. vanilla

Crust:
- 1 unbaked pie crust

Blend all filling ingredients and pour into unbaked pie crust. Bake at 350° for 30-35 minutes.

Mrs. Zeno Blattel
Kelso, Missouri
May 24, 1980

White Christmas Pie

- 2 baked 8-inch pie shells
- 1 can sweetened condensed milk
- ⅓ cup lemon juice
- ⅓ cup flaked coconut
- ½ cup chopped pecans
- 1 16-oz. can crushed pineapple, well-drained
- ½ tsp. pineapple flavoring
- 1 12- or 13-oz. tub whipped topping

Combine milk, lemon juice, coconut, pecans, pineapple and pineapple flavoring. Stir in whipped topping; pour mixture into pie shells. Chill at least 1 hour.

Edna Lines
Lamar, Missouri
November 29, 1985

■ A Bite to Eat ■

No matter what the time of day
Or who we chance to meet —
Seems one of us will always say
Let's have a bite to eat.
If you want a crowd just advertise
There's food that can't be beat.
An auction or garage sale —
Just have a bite to eat.
At every ladies gathering
Set tables nice and neat.
The minutes of the meeting read
And then a bite to eat.
Do you suppose when life is done
And we enter Pearly Gates
A form drifts up in flowing robes —
Offering a bite to eat?

— Mrs. George WessenDorf

168

Banana Split Pie

Turn a favorite dessert into a new pie idea.

½ cup butter OR margarine, softened
1½ cups sifted powdered sugar
2 eggs
1 tsp. vanilla
3 medium-size ripe bananas
1 1-oz. square chocolate, grated
¼ cup chopped walnuts
1 baked pie shell, cooled

Beat butter until creamy; add powdered sugar gradually, beating until light and fluffy. Add eggs 1 at a time, beating 3 minutes after each addition. Blend in vanilla. Peel and slice 2 bananas. Fold bananas and chocolate into powdered sugar mixture. Turn into cooled, baked pie shell. Sprinkle with walnuts. Chill 2-3 hours. Just before serving, peel and slice a banana and arrange on top of pie.

Ruth File
Superior, Nebraska
March 29, 1994

German's Chocolate Pie

This is a favorite of ours.

1 4-oz. chunk German's sweet chocolate
¼ cup butter, softened
1 13-oz. can evaporated milk
1 3½-oz. can flaked coconut
½ cup granulated sugar
3 large eggs, lightly beaten
½ cup chopped pecans, optional
1 tsp. vanilla
1 deep 9-inch pie crust, unbaked

Melt chocolate and butter together in saucepan over low heat. Add milk, coconut, granulated sugar and eggs. Mix well; then add pecans and vanilla. Pour into pie crust. Bake in 350° oven for 30 minutes or until knife inserted in center comes out clean. Serve pie warm with a scoop of vanilla ice cream.

Chris Bryant
Johnson City, Tennessee
June 19, 1990

Apple Butter Pie

I think you'll like this pie.

Crust:

- 1 cup all-purpose flour
- ½ tsp. salt
- ¼ cup margarine, chilled and cut into 8 pieces
- 3 Tbsps. vegetable shortening
- ½ cup shredded sharp Cheddar cheese
- 3-3½ Tbsps. ice cold water

Filling:

- 3 large eggs
- ⅓ cup light brown sugar, firmly packed
- ½ tsp. cinnamon
- ¼ tsp. salt
- • dash of ground cloves
- • dash of nutmeg
- • dash of allspice
- 1½ cups apple butter
- 1½ cups half-and-half

Crust: In large bowl, mix flour and salt. With pastry blender or 2 knives, cut in margarine, shortening and shredded cheese until mixture resembles coarse meal. Stir in ice cold water, 1 tablespoon at a time, until mixture begins to form a ball. Knead dough gently 2 or 3 times; flatten into disk shape. Dust with flour; wrap in waxed paper and chill 1 hour.

Roll out dough to make 11- to 12-inch circle; fit into 9-inch pie pan and trim, leaving 1-inch overhang. Dampen underside of edge with water, turn under and decorate with fork tines.

Filling: Combine eggs, brown sugar, cinnamon, salt, cloves, nutmeg and allspice. Beat with fork until well blended. Stir in apple butter and half-and-half until blended. Pour into pie crust. Bake in preheated 425° oven for 12 minutes, reduce heat to 350° and bake for 40 minutes more until filling is set. Remove from oven; cool on rack. Makes 8 servings.

Dorothy Bohling
Wichita, Kansas
November 6, 1990

NO SOGGY CRUSTS

To keep the bottom crust of a fruit pie from getting soggy, either pre-bake it partially or totally, or sprinkle some cake crumbs or bread crumbs into the bottom underneath the fruit. The crumbs will absorb some of the moisture from the fruit.

Sugarless Apple Pie

This is a nutritious pie using apples and apple juice.

- pastry for 9-inch double crust pie
- 6 medium Red Delicious apples, peeled and sliced
- 1 6-oz. can frozen apple juice (without sugar), thawed
- 1½ Tbsps. cornstarch
- ⅓ cup water
- 1 tsp. cinnamon
- 3 Tbsps. margarine

Place apples and undiluted apple juice into a large pan. Bring to a boil; reduce heat and simmer, covered, for about 5 minutes.

Dissolve cornstarch in water. Gently stir cornstarch into apple mixture. Bring to a boil; reduce heat and simmer, covered, for 10-15 minutes or until apples begin to soften. Stir in cinnamon.

Fill pastry shell with apples and cover with top crust. Bake at 350° for 45 minutes. Baste with melted margarine after baking.

Mrs. Lucile Anderson
Lathrop, Missouri
October 23, 1990

Caramel Pecan Pie

Very rich, but is a cool summer dessert. No oven heating!

- 1 envelope unflavored gelatin
- ¼ cup cold water
- ½ lb. vanilla caramels
- ¾ cup milk
- dash of salt
- 1 cup heavy cream, whipped
- ½ cup chopped pecans
- graham cracker crust

Soften gelatin in cold water. Melt caramels in milk over double boiler. Add softened gelatin and salt; stir well. Chill until slightly set. Then fold in whipped cream and chopped nuts. Pour mixture into graham cracker crust. Chill until firm, then serve.

Lois Wardrip
Bethany, Missouri
June 30, 1964

■ Mama's Cooking ■

She seldom used a recipe
Made everything from scratch,
A little bit of this 'n' that
She'd add to every batch.
She had no 'lectric blenders
No fancy mix machines;
Chopped, cut and peeled and pared
Onions, plums and beans.
Grew the herbs in summertime,
To flavor stews and hams;
Garlic flavored every dish,
Brown sugar sweetened yams.
She baked delicious fruit cakes
Each year at Christmas time,
Wrapped them in a dish towel
Soaked in dark, red wine.
Once frosted they were set aside
And saved for company;
Served dainty slices to her guests
When they dropped in for tea.
But my favorite dish of all
With certainty, I say
Was stuffin' Mama served to us
On each Thanksgiving Day.

— Angie Monnens

Appetizers and Extras

■ Appetizers and Extras ■

Spiced Honey Roasted Peanuts 175
Smoky Almond Cheese Ball 175
Bread Bear with Clam Dip 176
Coconut-Chicken Bites 177
Cheese Nuggets 177
Stuffed Rice Croquettes 178
Welcome Wafers 178
Vegetable Bars 179
Freezer Tomato Salsa 179
Raw Apple Relish 180
Green Tomato-Pepper Relish 180
Pickled Carrot Sticks 181
Lotweerick (Amish Dutch Apple Butter) 181
Green Tomato Jam 182
Zucchini Marmalade 182
Pear Mincemeat 183
Easy Strawberry Jam 183
Cherry-Rhubarb Jam 184
Rhubarb-Orange Jam 184
Old-Fashioned Citrus Aroma 184

■ Cedar Churn ■

Grandmother's cedar churn
conspicuous
in the dining room,
a reminder
of a bygone era
when the up-and-down
splash of the dash
brought forth
buttermilk
silky smooth,
with little bits
of floating butter,
and a tangy tongue
teasing taste of smooth
remembering.

— Ossie E. Tranbarger

Spiced Honey Roasted Peanuts

Unless you can find honey roasted peanuts on sale, they are costly. I'd like to share this recipe.

2   Tbsps. butter, melted
2   Tbsps. honey
2   tsps. minced garlic
1   tsp. ground red pepper
1   tsp. ground ginger
1   tsp. salt
1   lb. raw, skinned peanuts

Preheat oven to 325°. In medium bowl, combine all ingredients except peanuts. Add nuts and stir well. Spread in shallow baking pan and roast for 25 minutes, stirring once or twice. Cool. Makes 3 cups, 60 calories per table-spoon. Can be made ahead. Store in airtight container at room temperature up to 1 week.

Clara Young
Oxford, Kansas
January 2, 1990

Smoky Almond Cheese Ball

This is good served with rye snack bread or crackers.

1   7¾-oz. can red salmon OR chunk chicken
1   8-oz. pkg. cream cheese, softened
½   tsp. Liquid Smoke
2   Tbsps. chopped green pepper
1   Tbsp. chopped pimento
1   Tbsp. snipped parsley
½   cup sliced almonds, toasted

Coarsely chop ¼ cup almonds. Set aside. Flake salmon, removing bones and skin. Add cheese, Liquid Smoke, green peppers, pimento, parsley and chopped almonds. Shape into ball and roll in remaining ¼ cup sliced almonds. Chill 1 hour before serving. Makes a 3½-inch ball.

Mrs. O. Petersen
Utica, South Dakota
September 26, 1989

Bread Bear with Clam Dip

2   loaves frozen wheat OR white bread dough, thawed
3   black gumdrops
3   red gumdrops
•   thin (stringlike) black licorice, approx. 3 inches
1   tsp. honey OR light corn syrup

Clam Dip:
1   8-oz. pkg. cream cheese, softened
1   16-oz. carton sour cream
2   cloves fresh garlic, crushed
2   green onions, finely diced
1   6.5-oz. can chopped clams, drained
2   Tbsps. chopped fresh parsley
2   dashes of Worcestershire sauce
1   tsp. lemon juice
½   tsp. paprika

Shape 1 loaf of dough into a circle to form the bear's body. Place this round on a large greased baking sheet. Set aside. Take ⅔ of second loaf of dough and shape into a circle to form the bear's head. Place this round on a baking sheet next to the larger circle of dough so that they are touching; flatten both slightly.

Take the remaining ⅓ of dough and divide into 7 even pieces. Roll 4 of these into individual balls and attach each piece to sides of body for upper and lower paws. Take 2 of the remaining pieces and attach 1 piece to each side of bear's head for ears. Take the remaining piece of dough and shape into a circle 2½ inches in diameter. Attach this piece to the middle of the face.

Let the bear rise until double. Bake in preheated 375° oven for approximately 20-30 minutes or until golden brown and hollow sounding when tapped on top. If bear is browning too quickly, cover with foil and continue baking.

While bear is baking, make dip. Whip up cream cheese with beater. Add remaining ingredients, mix thoroughly, cover and place in refrigerator to enhance the flavor.

When bear has finished baking, remove it from baking sheet to cool on a wire rack. When cool, cut out a circle 6 inches in diameter from crust of bear's belly, being careful not to cut all the way through. Hollow out belly. When ready to serve, fill belly with dip. To decorate, use 2 black gumdrops for eyes, 1 black gumdrop for nose. Using black string licorice, make a mouth on the circle beneath the nose. You may need to use a bit of honey or corn syrup to attach eyes, nose and mouth. Attach a Christmas bow around neck. Red gumdrops or olives may be used for the 3 buttons down belly on dip if desired. Serve with bread slices, crackers or vegetables.

Kate Marchbanks Food Story December 3, 1991

Coconut-Chicken Bites

An unusual appetizer for holiday parties.

4   ozs. cream cheese, softened
2   Tbsps. mayonnaise
1   cup chopped, cooked chicken
1   cup blanched, chopped almonds
1   Tbsp. chopped chutney
½   tsp. salt
1   tsp. curry powder
½   cup toasted coconut

Combine cream cheese, mayonnaise, chopped chicken, almonds, chutney, salt and curry powder. Shape into small balls and roll in toasted coconut. Chill.

Makes about 4 dozen small appetizers.

Helen Nilan
Washington, Ohio
November 23, 1993

Cheese Nuggets

These would be good to serve during the holidays.

1   8-oz. pkg. cream cheese
2   2½-oz. pkgs. blue cheese
1   2½-oz. can deviled ham
¼   cup finely chopped pecans
⅛   tsp. onion powder
1/16 tsp. OR pinch of smoked salt
1   cup finely chopped parsley

Bring cream and blue cheeses to room temperature and mix together. Add deviled ham, pecans, onion powder and smoked salt. Chill until very firm. Shape into bite-size balls. Roll in parsley and chill thoroughly. Just before serving, insert wooden picks or small straight pretzel sticks into each ball. Makes 3-3½ dozen.

Helene Belanger
Denver, Colorado
November 20, 1990

Stuffed Rice Croquettes

These croquettes may be served hot as a side dish with meat or fowl, or served as a dessert simply by rolling in powdered sugar.

¼ lb. rice
1 lb. ricotta cheese
2 eggs, thoroughly beaten
1 cup bread crumbs
½ cup oil
• salt to taste

Cook rice. Spread 1 tablespoon of rice on palm of hand, add 1 tablespoon of ricotta cheese over rice, sprinkle with salt, top with more rice. Shape into round or oblong croquettes. Dip croquettes into well-beaten egg and roll in bread crumbs. Fry in very hot oil about 3 minutes or until golden brown.

**Vincent Argondezzi
Norristown, Pennsylvania
July 7, 1992**

Welcome Wafers

Seasoned crackers go well with fresh vegetables.

¼ cup butter, softened
½ cup shredded Cheddar cheese
⅓ cup blue cheese, crumbled
2 cups flour
½ clove garlic, minced
1 tsp. snipped parsley
1 tsp. snipped chives

Cream butter, Cheddar and blue cheese. Mix in flour, garlic, parsley and chives. Shape into 1½-inch rolls; chill. Slice and bake at 375° for 8-10 minutes.

**Mildred Sherrer
Bay City, Texas
August 2, 1994**

■ Time for a Change ■

*Summer lingers like a guest
who's stayed too long,
boring as the locusts'
droning monotone.
We crave October's tang,
air apple crisp, tart-sweet.
Autumn approaches,
ambling with dragging feet.*

— Billie Marsh

Vegetable Bars

These are good for lunch or a snack.

2   8-roll cans refriger-
     ated crescent rolls
¾   cup salad dressing
½   cup sour cream
2   8-oz. pkgs. cream
     cheese, softened
1   envelope ranch
     dressing mix
¾   cup chopped green
     pepper
¾   cup sliced green
     onion
¾   cup diced tomato
¾   cup chopped
     broccoli
¾   cup shredded carrot
¾   cup chopped
     cauliflower
•   shredded Cheddar
     cheese

Cover bottom of 7x11-inch pan with crescent rolls. Bake at 350° for 7-9 minutes and let cool. Mix salad dressing, sour cream, cream cheese and ranch dressing mix. Spread over crust. Combine vegetables and spread over dressing. Sprinkle with cheese. Cover with plastic wrap and press vegetables into dressing. Refrigerate covered for 3-4 hours or overnight. Cut into bars.

Virginia Garrelts
Salina, Kansas
September 27, 1994

Freezer Tomato Salsa

This is delicious for a chip dip or any recipe needing salsa.

12   large tomatoes
2   large onions
2   cloves minced garlic
¼   cup salad oil
1   12-oz. can tomato
     paste
2   envelopes instant
     beef broth
2   tsps. basil
2   tsps. salt
2   Tbsps. oregano
3   bay leaves
¼   cup granulated
     sugar
1   tsp. black pepper
2   cups water

Sauté chopped onions and garlic in oil until translucent. Wash tomatoes, cut out center core. Blend in blender. Add to onions and garlic. Cook 5 more minutes. Add tomato paste, beef broth, basil, salt, oregano, bay leaves, granulated sugar, pepper and water. Simmer for 1 hour. Cool completely and pour into freezer containers.

Iola Egle
McCook, Nebraska
September 15,1992

Raw Apple Relish

This relish adds gusto when served with baked fish or roast pork.

2   large apples, peeled and cored
¼   cup cauliflower, raw, cleaned and washed
1   raw carrot
¼   medium onion
¼   green pepper
¼   red pepper
2   Tbsps. lemon juice
¼   tsp. powdered ginger
•   salt and pepper to taste

Chop the apples, cauliflower, carrot, onion and peppers very, very fine, then blend. Add all other ingredients and mix well. Refrigerate for 1 hour before serving. Yields 2 cups.

Violet Beard
Marshall, Illinois
September 28, 1993

Green Tomato-Pepper Relish

4   qts. green tomatoes
½   cup salt
4   green peppers
1   red pepper
4   onions
4   cups white vinegar
2   cups granulated sugar
½   tsp. cinnamon
½   tsp. nutmeg
½   tsp. cloves
½   tsp. allspice

Slice washed tomatoes into crock, sprinkle with salt. Let stand overnight. Drain. Rinse and drain. Grind tomatoes, peppers and onion. Boil vinegar and granulated sugar; add remaining ingredients and boil 5 more minutes, then simmer over very low heat for 2 hours. Makes 3 quarts of relish.

Mrs. H.W. Walker
Richmond, Virginia
August 2, 1994

■ Apple Jelly ■

Today I made apple jelly
And I thought of a day when
We gathered wine red apples
Under the apple tree.

I thought of apple cider
Our grandpa used to make.
I thought of a day when mother
Made apple-dapple cake.

I thought of a copper kettle
Full of butter, golden brown,

Pickled Carrot Sticks

I think you will like these.

- 6 medium carrots
- 1 cup vinegar
- 1 cup water
- ⅓ cup granulated sugar
- ⅛ tsp. pepper
- 1 tsp. whole mixed spices
- ½ tsp. salt

Wash and scrape carrots. Simmer in saltwater until almost tender. Drain and cut into sticks. Combine vinegar, water, granulated sugar, pepper, whole spices and salt. Boil for 2 minutes. Put carrot sticks in jars and pour vinegar mixture over top. Keep refrigerated.

Carrie Treichel
Johnson City, Tennessee
October 22, 1991

Lotweerick (Amish Dutch Apple Butter)

This is just delicious!

- 4 qts. sliced apples
- 2 qts. water
- 1½ qts. cider
- 1½ lbs. granulated sugar
- 1 tsp. cinnamon
- 1 tsp. allspice
- 1 tsp. cloves

Wash and slice apples. Cover with water and boil until soft. Press through sieve to remove skins and seeds. Bring cider to boil, add apple pulp and granulated sugar; cook until it thickens, stirring constantly. Add spices; cook until thick enough to spread. Pour into sterilized jars and seal.

Editor's Note: Pint jars should be processed in boiling water bath for 10 minutes.

Mrs. H.W. Walker
Richmond, Virginia
October 24, 1989

With an old time, handmade paddle
To stir it 'round and 'round.

I thought of apple dumplings
And deep dish apple pie.
I thought of apple orchards
And swallows in the sky.

I just couldn't keep from thinking
While I bottled my jelly down,
Of the fragrant, old time sweetness
Of apples all around.

— Verna Sparks

Green Tomato Jam

This is simple and delicious.

2 qts. green
  tomatoes, sliced
½ tsp. salt
4 cups granulated
  sugar
4 lemons, sliced thin
• enough water to
  cover tomatoes
2 sticks cinnamon

Boil tomatoes, salt, granulated sugar and lemons in water for 10 minutes. Remove from heat; add cinnamon. Simmer 45 minutes, until thick.

Mrs. Carl Diecker
Duncan, Oklahoma
August 16, 1994

Zucchini Marmalade

A super recipe and a good way to use those overlooked zucchini that seem to hide in our gardens. This keeps in the refrigerator like uncooked strawberry jam.

6 cups zucchini (large
  ones), shredded
½ cup lemon juice
6 cups granulated
  sugar
1 cup crushed pine-
  apple with juice
1 large pkg. OR 2
  small pkgs. apricot
  gelatin

Peel and remove seeds from zucchini. Shred, then cook or simmer slowly on low heat, stirring often. Add lemon juice, granulated sugar, pineapple and gelatin; cook 6 minutes. Pour into sterile jars. Makes 8 half pints. Store in refrigerator.

Florence Miller
Des Moines, Iowa
August 30, 1994

Pear Mincemeat

I have used this tasty recipe for years.

6 lbs. pears
4 lbs. apples
2 small oranges
2 lbs. raisins
1 12-oz. can crushed pineapple
1 Tbsp. salt
1 tsp. cinnamon
½ tsp. cloves
5 cups granulated sugar

Stem and core pears and apples, but don't peel. Quarter oranges to remove seeds, but don't remove peel. Chop or grind pears, apples and oranges in food chopper, saving all the juice. Mix chopped fruit, fruit juice, raisins, pineapple, salt, cinnamon, cloves and granulated sugar in large pan, stirring to mix well. Cook at high heat until mixture boils, then reduce heat. Continue to boil for 1 hour on low heat. Seal in hot sterilized jars with lids. This mincemeat will keep indefinitely. More spices or granulated sugar may be added to suit taste.

Mrs. R.R. Rowton
Bartlesville, Oklahoma
September 13, 1994

Easy Strawberry Jam

2 cups mashed strawberries
4 cups granulated sugar OR 3 cups granulated sugar and 1 cup honey
1 pkg. fruit pectin
¾ cup water

Mix strawberries and granulated sugar thoroughly; set aside 10 minutes. Stir fruit pectin with water in saucepan. Bring to a boil, stirring constantly. Boil 1 minute; remove from heat. Stir mixtures together until granulated sugar is completely dissolved and no longer grainy. Pour into plastic containers; cover with tight lids. Let stand at room temperature 24 hours. Store in freezer. After opening, store in refrigerator. Makes about four 8-oz. containers.

Kate Marchbanks Food Story
June 4, 1991

Cherry-Rhubarb Jam

A good way to use rhubarb is in a delicious jam. We like this very much.

5 cups rhubarb, finely cut
1 cup water
5 cups granulated sugar
1 can cherry pie filling
2 3-oz. pkgs. cherry gelatin

Cook rhubarb in water until tender. Add granulated sugar and cook a few minutes, stirring constantly. Add pie filling and cook 6-8 minutes more. Remove from heat and add gelatin. Stir until completely dissolved. Pour into jars and seal. Store in refrigerator or freezer.

Alma James
Maywood, California
September 26, 1985

Rhubarb-Orange Jam

I wrote Capper's *Lost and Found column asking for this recipe a while back. Since you didn't have the recipe, I want to share it with your readers.*

5 cups finely cut and well-packed rhubarb
3½ cups granulated sugar
1 lb. orange slice candy, sliced fine
• few drops red food coloring

Mix rhubarb and granulated sugar together. Boil 5 minutes. Add sliced orange slices and boil 5 minutes more. Add a few drops of food coloring to give jam a pretty color. Place in sterilized jars and seal.

Lorraine Cagle
Long Beach, Washington
July 4, 1989

Old-Fashioned Citrus Aroma

When preparing recipes using grapefruit, lemons and oranges, do not discard the rinds. Save in a container in the refrigerator and later make this citrus potpourri.

4 cups water
2 sticks cinnamon
1 Tbsp. cloves
1 Tbsp. allspice
• peel of 1 grapefruit
• peel of 2 lemons
• peel of 2 oranges

Bring to a boil in a kettle and let simmer as long as needed to perfume the house. This may be used more than once. Just refrigerated between uses.

Karen Ann Bland
Gove, Kansas
December 21, 1993

■ The Mother's Apples ■

My daughter, who knew little of money,
said no, don't buy the dollar basket of apples;
they might have worms.
Unwilling to take a chance.

They looked OK to me.
Worms can be cut
out, I said.

She wrinkled her nose and turned away.
Too cheap.

I soaked the apples overnight, pared
them at the sink. No worms were cut
but a bruise or so. So what?

The stove was heated low, the water
mixed with cinnamon.

She came down from her room
and asked what smelled so good.
The rich aroma of cheap apples
sailed through the house.

I hoped she learned it's not the cost
when living life or making applesauce
that is always the most important.

— **Lynette G. Esposito**

■ Jam Session ■

Little jars
of summer:
sugary, strawberried
fingers
mixing winter's
tart-sweet memories
of freshly-flavored
sunshiny days
for toast
on frosty
morns.

— **Pearl Bloch Segall**

NUTRIENT CONTENT LABELING CLAIMS DEFINITIONS

Descriptive Term	Definition by Food Energy/Nutrient Category						Comments
	Calories	Fat	Sat. Fat	Choles.	Sodium	Sugars	
Free	Contains no amount of, or only trivial amounts of, any one or more of the categories: calories, fat, saturated fat, cholesterol, sodium, and sugars.						Synonyms: "no," "zero," "without"
	<5 kcal/ serving	<0.5 g/ serving	<0.5 g/ serving	<2 mg/ serving	<5 mg/ serving	<0.5 g/ serving	
Low	40 kcal or less/ serving	3 g or less/ serving	1 g or less/ serving	20 mg or less/ serving	140 mg or less/ serving	Not defined	Synonyms: "little," ("few" for calories), Amount applies/50 g food if refer-enced amount 30 g or less (small serving)
Very Low					35 mg or less/ serving		
Lean		<10 g/ serving	<4 g/ serving	<95 mg/ serving			Amounts apply per 100 g also
Extra Lean		<5 g/ serving	<2 g/ serving	<95 mg/ serving			Amounts apply per 100 g also
Light or Lite	contains 1/3 fewer calories than ref. food	contains 1/2 fat of ref. food			content reduced by 50% in low-calorie/ low-fat food		If food gets 50% or more of calories from fat, must have 50% reduction in fat
Reduced	Nutritionally altered product has at least 25% less of nutrient or calories than reference product. Claim can't be made if reference food meets requirement for "low" claim.						Synonyms: "lower," ("fewer" for calories)
Less	Food, altered or not, has 25% less of a nutrient or calories per reference serving.						Synonym: "fewer"
High	Contains 20% or more of DC for nutrient per reference serving.						
More	Food, altered or not, has 10% or more of DV of nutrient per reference serving.						
Good Source	10-19% of DV of a particular nutrient per reference servings.						
Fresh	May only be used on a food that is raw, never frozen or heated and contains no preservatives.						

TABLE OF EQUIVALENTS

ABBREVIATIONS AND SYMBOLS*

CAPACITY
Cup (c)
Deciliter (d)
Fluid ounce (fl oz)
Gallon (gal)
Liter (l)
Milliliter (ml)
Pint (pt)
Quart (qt)
Peck (pk)
Bushel (bu)
Gill (gi)
Tablespoon (Tbsp)
Teaspoon (tsp)

TIME
Hour (hr)
Minute (min)
Second (sec)

TEMPERATURE
Degrees Celsius (°C)
Degrees Fahrenheit (°F)

LENGTH
Centimeter (cm)
Foot (ft)
Inch (in)
Meter (m)
Millimeter (mm)
Millimicron (mu)

WEIGHT
Gram (g)
Kilogram (kg)
Microgram (ug)
Milligram (mg)
Ounce (oz)
Pound (lb)

* Note that abbreviations are used in the singular form regardless of whether the item is singular or plural. For metric units a symbol is used, as g for grams.

WEIGHT AND VOLUME EQUIVALENTS

COMMON UNITS OF WEIGHT
1 gram	=	0.035 ounces
1 kilogram	=	2.21 pounds
1 ounce	=	28.35 grams
1 pound	=	453.59 grams

COMMON UNITS OF VOLUME
1 bushel	=	4 pecks
1 peck	=	8 quarts
1 gallon	=	4 quarts
1 quart	=	2 pints
	=	946.4 milliliters
1 pint	=	2 cups
1 cup	=	16 tablespoons
	=	2 gills
	=	8 fluid ounces
	=	236.6 milliliters
1 Tablespoon	=	3 teaspoons
	=	1/2 fluid ounce
	=	14.8 milliliters
1 teaspoon	=	4.9 milliliters
1 liter	=	1000 milliliters
	=	1.06 quarts

EQUIVALENTS FOR ONE UNIT AND FRACTIONS OF A UNIT

TABLESPOON
1 Tbsp = 3 tsp
7/8 Tbsp = 2 1/2 tsp
3/4 Tbsp = 2 1/4 tsp
2/3 Tbsp = 2 tsp
5/8 Tbsp = 1 7/8 tsp
1/2 Tbsp = 1 1/2 tsp
3/8 Tbsp = 1 1/8 tsp
1/3 Tbsp = 1 tsp
1/4 Tbsp = 3/4 tsp

QUART
1 qt = 2 pt
7/8 qt = 3 1/2 c
3/4 qt = 3 c
2/3 qt = 2 2/3 c
5/8 qt = 2 1/2 c
1/2 qt = 1 pt
3/8 qt = 1 1/2 c
1/3 qt = 1 1/3 c
1/4 qt = 1 c
1/8 qt = 1/2 c
1/16 qt = 1/4 c

CUP
1 c = 16 Tbsp
7/8 c = 14 Tbsp
3/4 c = 12 Tbsp
2/3 c = 10 2/3 Tbsp
5/8 c = 10 Tbsp
1/2 c = 8 Tbsp
3/8 c = 6 Tbsp
1/3 c = 5 1/3 Tbsp
1/4 c = 4 Tbsp
1/8 c = 2 Tbsp
1/16 c = 1 Tbsp

GALLON
1 gal = 4 qt
7/8 gal = 3 1/2 qt
3/4 gal = 3 qt
2/3 gal = 10 2/3 c
5/8 gal = 5 pt
1/2 gal = 2 qt
3/8 gal = 3 pt
1/3 gal = 5 1/3 c
1/4 gal = 1 qt
1/8 gal = 1 pt
1/16 gal = 1 c

PINT
1 pt = 2 c
7/8 pt = 1 3/4 c
3/4 pt = 1 1/2 c
2/3 pt = 1 1/3 c
5/8 pt = 1 1/4 c
1/2 pt = 1 c
3/8 pt = 3/4 c
1/3 pt = 2/3 c
1/4 pt = 1/2 c
1/8 pt = 1/4 c
1/16 pt = 2 Tbsp

POUND
1 lb = 16 oz
7/8 lb = 14 oz
3/4 lb = 12 oz
2/3 lb = 10 2/3 oz
5/8 lb = 10 oz
1/2 lb = 8 oz
3/8 lb = 6 oz
1/3 lb = 5 1/3 oz
1/4 lb = 4 oz
1/8 lb = 2 oz
1/16 lb = 1 oz

Information reprinted with permission from the *Handbook of Food Preparation*.

Cook's Notes

Cook's Notes

Cook's Notes

Index

∎ A ∎

Almond Cheese Ball, Smoky 175
Apple
   Apple Butter Bread 12
   Apple Butter Pie 170
   Apple Doughnuts 23
   Apple-Orange Pie 157
   Apple Pie Cake 108
   Butter Pecan Apple Pie 164
   Caramel Apples 141
   Lotweerick
   (Amish Dutch Apple Butter) 181
   Quick Apple Bread 13
   Raw Apple Relish 180
   Skillet Apple Cake 131
   Sugarless Apple Pie 171
   Topsy Turvy Apple Pecan Pie . . .167
Apricot
   Apricot Nuggets 31
   Dried Apricot Cranberry Tart 142
Artichoke
   Artichoke Salad 101
   Kathie's Artichoke Bake 80
Asparagus
   Asparagus Salad 102
   Chicken Breasts
   with Asparagus 76

∎ B ∎

Baby Food Cake 126
Baked Cabbage Casserole 90
Baked Chicken Breasts
with Cranberry Sauce 77
Baked Chicken Puff 76
Banana
   Banana Macadamia
   Nut Bread 10
   Banana Split Pie 169
   Moist Banana Bundt Cake 110
Bars
   Butterscotch
   Cheesecake Bars 44
   Chelsea's Choco-Nutty
   Crunch Bars 47
   Chocolate Crispy Bars 51
   Cranberry Cheesecake Bars 50
   Disappearing
   Marshmallow Bars 38

Double Chocolate
Crumble Bars 53
Frosted Jam Bars 38
Soft Date Bars 39
Spicy Pumpkin Bars
with Cream Cheese Icing 140
True Goodie Bars 40
Vegetable Bars 179
Zucchini Bars 42
Beans
   Beans and Meatballs 62
   Curried Bean and Rice Salad 95
   Sausage Apple Bean Bake 71
   Swedish Bean Bake 89
Beef Pot Roast, Horseradish 64
Beet Salad 98
Best-Ever Turkey Casserole 75
Best Rhubarb Shortcake 126
Biscuits
   Country Ham Biscuits 24
   Sweet Potato Biscuits 23
Black Forest Cake 133
Black Walnut Cake 113
Blackberry Cobbler 141
Blueberry Poppy Seed
Brunch Cake 109
Blueberry Surprise Cake 129
Bonbons, Fudgy 27
Brazilian Custard 144
Breads
   Apple Butter Bread 12
   Banana Macadamia
   Nut Bread 10
   Bread Bear with Clam Dip 176
   Cranberry-Walnut Loaf 11
   Easy Microwave Pizza Breads . . .69
   Eggnog Bread 16
   English Muffin Loaves 9
   Irish Freckle Bread 9
   Lime Tea Bread 16
   Low Cholesterol Bran Bread 15
   Momovers 24
   Pear Bread 14
   Pecan Bread 14
   Poppy Seed Bread 17
   Pork and Bean Bread 13
   Quick Apple Bread 13
   Raspberry Cereal Bread 12
   Zucchini Bread 11
Broccoli-Cauliflower Salad 100

Broccoli Corn Bread 15
Broccoli Puff 94
Broccoli Salad 99
Broccoli Soup 87
Brown Sugar
Meringue Spice Cake 119
Brownies
 Cherry Chip Brownies 53
 York Brownies 48
Bun Candy .30
Butter Pecan Apple Pie 164
Butterscotch Cheesecake Bars 44

■ C ■

Cabbage
 Baked Cabbage Casserole 90
 Sweet-Sour Cabbage 103
Cakes
 Apple Pie Cake 108
 Baby Food Cake 126
 Best Rhubarb Shortcake 126
 Black Forest Cake 133
 Black Walnut Cake 113
 Blueberry Poppy Seed
 Brunch Cake 109
 Blueberry Surprise Cake 129
 Brown Sugar
 Meringue Spice Cake 119
 Champagne Cake 114
 Cherry Chocolate Cake 110
 Chocolate Beet Cake 123
 Chocolate-Caramel
 Poke and Pour Cake 120
 Chocolate Carrot Cake 113
 Chocolate Eclair Cake 115
 Chocolate Praline Layer Cake . . .111
 Cholesterol-Free
 Lemon Chiffon Cake 121
 Coke Cake with Icing 123
 Cold Oven Pound Cake 134
 Grandma West's
 Chocolate Cake 125
 Hawaiian Pineapple
 Poke Cake 118
 Mexican Chocolate
 Chiffon Cake 129
 Mississippi Mud Cake 117
 Moist Banana Bundt Cake 110
 My Ranch Cake 116
 Orange Dessert Cake 134
 Poppy Seed Cake 128
 Prince of Wales Cake 127
 Pumpkin Pie Cake 135
 Punch Bowl Cake 114
 Raisin Lemon Cake 118
 Rhubarb Custard Cake 107
 Rich and Delicious Cake 135

Skillet Apple Cake 131
Snow Mountain Cake 130
Sock-it-to-me Cake 132
Strawberry Soda Pop Cake 112
Unusual Frozen Cake 127
Vanilla Wafer Cake 131
Yuletide Eggnog Cake 122
Candy
 Apricot Nuggets 31
 Bun Candy 30
 Flake Candy 28
 Honey Candy 30
 Orange-Butterscotch
 Walnut Clusters 32
Caramel Apples 141
Caramel Pecan Cheesecake 132
Caramel Pecan Pie 171
Carrot
 Carrot-Chive Salad 101
 Pickled Carrot Sticks 181
Casserole
 Baked Cabbage Casserole 90
 Best-Ever Turkey Casserole 75
 Chicken Dressing Casserole 78
 Cranberry and
 Bean Casserole 70
 Good Morning Casserole 73
 Swiss Green Bean Casserole 92
 Yum-Yum Casserole 75
 Zucchini Beef Casserole 67
Cheese
 Cheese and Potato
 Wild Rice Soup 74
 Cheese and Sausage Bake 71
 Cheese Nuggets 177
 Cheese Spread Fudge 29
 Cottage Cheese Delight 150
 Smoky Almond Cheese Ball 175
Champagne Cake 114
Cheesecake
 Caramel Pecan
 Cheesecake 132
 Cherry Cheesecake 125
 Miniature Cheesecakes 119
Chelsea's Choco-Nutty
Crunch Bars 47
Cherry Angel Dessert 152
Cherry Cheesecake 125
Cherry Chip Brownies 53
Cherry Chocolate Cake 110
Cherry-Rhubarb Jam 184
Cherub Coins 43
Chicken
 Baked Chicken Breasts
 with Cranberry Sauce 77
 Baked Chicken Puff 76
 Chicken Breasts, Picnic Style 78

Chicken Breasts
with Asparagus 76
Chicken Dressing Casserole 78
Chicken Pot Pie 79
Coconut-Chicken Bites 177
Fruited Chicken Salad 97
Oven Barbecued Chicken 77
Quick Low-Fat
Raspberry Chicken 79
Thai Chicken
and Vegetable Salad 96
Chiffon Sweet Potato Pie 93
Chili, Restaurant 68
Chocolate
Chocolate Beet Cake 123
Chocolate-Caramel
Poke and Pour Cake 120
Chocolate Carrot Cake 113
Chocolate Crispy Bars 51
Chocolate Cream Pecan Pie 160
Chocolate Eclair Cake 115
Chocolate Malt Ball Cookies 54
Chocolate Pie 161
Chocolate Praline Layer Cake . . .111
Double Chocolate
Crumble Bars 53
German's Chocolate Pie 169
Grandma West's
Chocolate Cake 125
Mexican Chocolate
Chiffon Cake 129
Three-In-One Chocolate Torte . . .107
Cholesterol-Free
Lemon Chiffon Cake 121
Cobbler, Blackberry 141
Coconut-Chicken Bites 177
Coconut Cream
Dessert, Toasted 145
Coconut Crisps 41
Coconut Macaroon Cookies 45
Coffeecake
Cranberry Coffeecake 124
Overnight Coffeecake 22
Rhubarb Coffeecake 108
Coke Cake with Icing 123
Cold Oven Pound Cake 134
Coleslaw, Polynesian 100
Colonial Peanut Butter Fudge 28
Cookies
Cherub Coins 43
Chocolate Malt Ball Cookies 54
Coconut Crisps 41
Coconut Macaroon Cookies 45
Cowboy Cookies 45
'Cowless' Cow Patties 44
Dr. Pepper Snowballs 37
Gourmet Cookies 51

Hanukkah Gelt Cookies 56
Jumbo Cookies 46
Magic Peanut
Butter Cookies 49
Mincemeat Drop Cookies 43
Monster Cookies 50
Oatmeal Cookie Mix 40
Oatmeal Fruit Cookies 52
Oatmeal Lemon-
Cheese Cookies 55
Orange-Nut Balls 39
Peanut Butter Middles 42
Pineapple Oatmeal Drops 52
Pink Frosted Cookies 37
Praline Cookies 41
Roll 'n' Cut Cookies 48
Corn Bread
Broccoli Corn Bread 15
Corn Bread Salad 95
My Custard Corn Bread 17
Cottage Cheese Delight 150
Country Ham Biscuits 24
Cowboy Cookies 45
'Cowless' Cow Patties 44
Crafty Crescent Lasagne 66
Cranberry and
Bean Casserole 70
Cranberry Apple Crunch 145
Cranberry Cheesecake Bars 50
Cranberry Coffeecake 124
Cranberry Potato Puffs 151
Cranberry Pudding
with Butter Sauce 148
Cranberry-Walnut Loaf 11
Creamy Maple Praline Pie 159
Crock Pizza 69
Croquettes, Stuffed Rice 178
Cupcakes, Filled 120
Curried Bean and Rice Salad 95
Custard
Brazilian Custard 144
Custard's Last Stand 150
My Custard Corn Bread 17

▪ D ▪

Danggood Pie 166
Danish Limas 94
Date Bars, Soft 39
Desserts
Cherry Angel Dessert 152
Cottage Cheese Delight 150
Cranberry Apple Crunch 145
Custard's Last Stand 150
Dessert in a Pumpkin 142
Earthquake Dessert 153
Fruit Pizza 139
Layered Rhubarb Dessert 144

195

Lemon Delight 147
Potica 143
Sinfully Rich Dessert 151
Strawberry Fool 149
Strawberry Mousse 148
Strawberry Swirl 152
Toasted Coconut
Cream Dessert 145
Velvety Lime Squares 139
Disappearing
Marshmallow Bars 38
Divinity
Matilda's Divinity 31
Sorghum Divinity 29
Dorathea's Oat Muffins 19
Double Chocolate
Crumble Bars 53
Doughnuts
Apple Doughnuts 23
Oven Baked Doughnuts 22
Dr. Pepper Snowballs 37
Dried Apricot Cranberry Tart 142
Drumstick Ice Cream Pie 164
Dumplings, Peach 153

■ E ■

Earthquake Dessert 153
Easy Microwave
Pizza Breads 69
Easy Strawberry Jam 183
Eggnog
Eggnog Bread 16
Yuletide Eggnog Cake 122
Enchiladas, Seafood 82
English Muffin Loaves 9

■ F ■

Filled Cupcakes 120
Fish
Tuna Burgers 82
Tuna Cauliflower Fiesta 91
Tuna Rolls 81
Flake Candy 28
Freezer Tomato Salsa 179
Fresh Peach Pie 163
Frosted Jam Bars 38
Frozen Yogurt 147
Fruit Cocktail Parfait Pie 160
Fruit Pizza 139
Fruited Chicken Salad 97
Fudge
Cheese Spread Fudge 29
Colonial Peanut Butter Fudge 28
Two-Flavor Fudge 32
White Fruited Fudge 33
Fudgy Bonbons 27

■ G ■

German's Chocolate Pie 169
Gingered Pear-Topped
Mincemeat Pie 158
Good Morning Casserole 73
Gourmet Cookies 51
Grandma West's
Chocolate Cake 125
Granny's Angel Food Pie 158
Green Beans
Summer Green Bean Salad 104
Swiss Green Bean Casserole 92
Green Tomato Jam 182
Green Tomato-Pepper Relish 180
Greengage Plum Salad 99

■ H ■

Hanukkah Gelt Cookies 56
Hawaiian Pineapple
Poke Cake 118
Hearty Swirled
Meat Loaf with Cheese 63
Honey Candy 30
Horseradish Beef Pot Roast 64

■ I ■

Ice Cream
Drumstick Ice Cream Pie 164
Ice Cream Muffins 20
Impossible Taco Pie 59
Irish Freckle Bread 9

■ J ■

Jam
Cherry-Rhubarb Jam 184
Easy Strawberry Jam 183
Frosted Jam Bars 38
Green Tomato Jam 182
Rhubarb-Orange Jam 184
Jumbo Cookies 46

■ K ■

Kathie's Artichoke Bake 80

■ L ■

Lasagne
Crafty Crescent Lasagne 66
Lasagne .65
Layered Rhubarb Dessert 144
Lemon
Cholesterol-Free Lemon
Chiffon Cake 121
Lemon Delight 147
Lemon Poppy Seed Muffins 20

Limas, Danish 94
Lime
   Lime Tea Bread 16
   Velvety Lime Squares 139
Lotweerick
(Amish Dutch Apple Butter) 181
Low Cholesterol Bran Bread 15

▪ M ▪

Magic Peanut
Butter Cookies 49
Manicotti 72
Marmalade, Zucchini 182
Marshmallow Bars,
Disappearing 38
Marvelous Meatballs 62
Matilda's Divinity 31
Meatballs
   Beans and Meatballs 62
   Marvelous Meatballs 62
   Spaghetti and
   Meatballs, Family Style 61
   Swedish Meatballs 60
Meat Loaf
   Hearty Swirled
   Meat Loaf with Cheese 63
   Super Meat Loaf 64
Mexican Chocolate
Chiffon Cake 129
Mincemeat
   Gingered Pear-Topped
   Mincemeat Pie 158
   Mincemeat Drop Cookies 43
   Mincemeat Ice Cream Pie 161
   Pear Mincemeat 183
Miniature Cheesecakes 119
Mississippi Mud Cake 117
Moist Banana Bundt Cake 110
Momovers .24
Monster Cookies 50
Monterey Pizza Rice 74
Morning Glory Muffins 21
Mousse, Strawberry 148
Muffins
   Dorathea's Oat Muffins 19
   Ice Cream Muffins 20
   Lemon Poppy Seed Muffins 20
   Morning Glory Muffins 21
   Pumpkin-Oat Muffins 18
   Squash Muffins 19
   Strawberry-Rhubarb Muffins 18
My Custard Corn Bread 17
My Ranch Cake 116

▪ N ▪

Noodle Soup and Butter Balls 88

Nuggets
   Apricot Nugget 31
   Cheese Nuggets 177

▪ O ▪

Oat Muffins, Dorathea's 19
Oatmeal Cookie Mix 40
Oatmeal Fruit Cookies 52
Oatmeal-Lemon-
Cheese Cookies 55
Oatmeal Pie 168
Old-Fashioned Citrus Aroma 184
Old-Fashioned
Praline Pecan Rolls 21
Onion Pie .90
Orange-Butterscotch
Walnut Clusters 32
Orange Dessert Cake 134
Orange Nut Balls 39
Oven Baked Doughnuts 22
Oven Barbecued Chicken 77
Overnight Coffeecake 22

▪ P ▪

Peach
   Fresh Peach Pie 163
   Peach Dumplings 153
Peanut Butter
   Colonial Peanut Butter Fudge 28
   Magic Peanut Butter Cookies 49
   Peanut Butter Middles 42
   Peanut Butter Pie 162
Peanuts, Spiced Honey Roasted . .175
Pear Bread 14
Pear Mincemeat 183
Pecans
   Old-Fashioned
   Praline Pecan Rolls 21
   Pecan Bread 14
Pepsi Pork Roast 65
Pickled Carrot Sticks 181
Pies
   Apple Butter Pie 170
   Apple-Orange Pie 157
   Banana Split Pie 169
   Butter Pecan Apple Pie 164
   Caramel Pecan Pie 171
   Chicken Pot Pie 79
   Chiffon Sweet Potato Pie 93
   Chocolate Cream Pecan Pie 160
   Chocolate Pie 161
   Creamy Maple Praline Pie 159
   Danggood Pie 166
   Drumstick Ice Cream Pie 164
   Fresh Peach Pie 163
   Fruit Cocktail Parfait Pie 160

German's Chocolate Pie 169
Gingered Pear-Topped
  Mincemeat Pie 158
Granny's Angel Food Pie 158
Impossible Taco Pie 59
Mincemeat Ice Cream Pie 161
Oatmeal Pie 168
Onion Pie 90
Peanut Butter Pie 162
Reuben Pie 59
Rhubarb-and-Strawberry Pie 165
Shepherd's Pie 60
Strawberry-Pudding Pie 165
Sugarless Apple Pie 171
Topsy Turvy
  Apple Pecan Pie 167
Watermelon Chiffon Pie 166
White Christmas Pie 168
Wonderful Walnut Pie 162
Zucchini Pie 163
Pineapple
  Hawaiian Pineapple
    Poke Cake 118
  Pineapple Oatmeal Drops 52
Pink Frosted Cookies 37
Pizza
  Crock Pizza 69
  Easy Microwave
    Pizza Breads 69
  Fruit Pizza 139
  Monterey Pizza Rice 74
  Veggie Pizza 83
Plum Salad, Greengage 99
Polynesian Coleslaw 100
Poor Man's Steak 67
Poppy Seed Bread 17
Poppy Seed Cake 128
Pork
  Pepsi Pork Roast 65
  Pork and Bean Bread 13
  Sweet Barbecue Pork Chops 70
Potatoes
  Cranberry Potato Puffs 151
  Potato Supreme 88
  Reunion Scalloped Potatoes 92
  You Won't Believe
    It's Potato Salad 98
Potica 143
Pralines
  Creamy Maple Praline Pie 159
  Old-Fashioned
    Praline Pecan Rolls 21
    Praline Cookies 41
Prince of Wales Cake 127
Pudding
  Cranberry Pudding
    with Butter Sauce 148

Vegetable Pudding 91
Pumpkin
  Dessert in a Pumpkin 142
  Pumpkin-Oat Muffins 18
  Pumpkin Pie Cake 135
  Pumpkin Torte 146
  Spicy Pumpkin Bars
    with Cream Cheese Icing 140
Punch Bowl Cake 114

■ Q ■

Quick Apple Bread 13
Quick Low-Fat
  Raspberry Chicken 79

■ R ■

Raisin Lemon Cake 118
Raspberry
  Quick Low-Fat
    Raspberry Chicken 79
  Raspberry Cereal Bread 12
Relish
  Green Tomato-Pepper Relish . . .180
  Raw Apple Relish 180
Restaurant Chili 68
Reuben Pie 59
Reunion Scalloped Potatoes 92
Rhubarb
  Best Rhubarb Shortcake 126
  Layered Rhubarb Dessert 144
  Rhubarb-and-Strawberry Pie 165
  Rhubarb Coffeecake 108
  Rhubarb Custard Cake 107
  Rhubarb-Orange Jam 184
Rice
  Monterey Pizza Rice 74
  Rice Fruit Salad 103
  Stuffed Rice Croquettes 178
Rich and Delicious Cake 135
Roll 'n' Cut Cookies 48

■ S ■

Salads
  Artichoke Salad 101
  Asparagus Salad 102
  Beet Salad 98
  Broccoli-Cauliflower Salad 100
  Broccoli Salad 99
  Carrot-Chive Salad 101
  Corn Bread Salad 95
  Curried Bean and Rice Salad 95
  Fruited Chicken Salad 97
  Greengage Plum Salad 99
  Rice Fruit Salad 103
  Shoestring Salad 97
  Spinach-Orange Salad 102

198

Summer Green Bean Salad 104
Thai Chicken
and Vegetable Salad 96
You Won't Believe
It Isn't Potato Salad 98
Salsa, Freezer Tomato 179
Sausage
    Cheese and Sausage Bake 71
    Sausage Apple Bean Bake 71
Scrapple 73
Seafood Enchilidas 82
Shepherd's Pie 60
Shoestring Salad 97
Sinfully Rich Dessert 151
Skillet Apple Cake 131
Smoky Almond Cheese Ball 175
Snow Mountain Cake 130
Sock-it-to-me Cake 132
Soft Date Bars 39
Sorghum Divinity 29
Soup
    Broccoli Soup 87
    Cheese and Potato
    Wild Rice Soup 74
    Noodle Soup
    and Butter Balls 88
Spaghetti and
Meatballs, Family Style 61
Spiced Honey Roasted Peanuts ...175
Spicy Pumpkin Bars
with Cream Cheese Icing 140
Spinach-Orange Salad 102
Squash
    Squash Muffins 19
    Summer Squash Surprise 89
Steak, Poor Man's 67
Strawberry
    Easy Strawberry Jam 183
    Strawberry Fool 149
    Strawberry Mousse 148
    Strawberry-Pudding Pie 165
    Strawberry-Rhubarb Muffins 18
    Strawberry Soda Pop Cake 112
    Strawberry Swirl 152
Stuffed Rice Croquettes 178
Sugarless Apple Pie 171
Summer Green Bean Salad 104
Summer Squash Surprise 89
Super Meat Loaf 64
Swedish Bean Bake 89
Swedish Meatballs 60
Sweet Barbecue Pork Chops 70
Sweet Potato
    Chiffon Sweet Potato Pie 93
    Sweet Potato Biscuits 23
Sweet-Sour Cabbage 103
Swiss Green Bean Casserole 92

■ T ■

Tart, Dried Apricot Cranberry 142
Thai Chicken
and Vegetable Salad 96
Three-In-One Chocolate Torte 107
Toasted Coconut Cream Dessert ..145
Tomato
    Freezer Tomato Salsa 179
    Tomato Aspic Extraordinaire 104
Topsy Turvy Apple Pecan Pie 167
Torte
    Pumpkin Torte 146
    Three-in-One Chocolate Torte ...107
Tuna Burgers 82
Tuna Cauliflower Fiesta 91
Tuna Rolls 81
True Goodie Bars 40
Turkey Casserole, Best-Ever 75
Two-Flavored Fudge 32

■ U ■

Unusual Frozen Cake 127

■ V ■

Vanilla Wafer Cake 131
Velvety Lime Squares 139

■ W ■

Watermelon Chiffon Pie 166
Welcome Wafers 178
White Christmas Pie 168
White Fruited Fudge 33
Wonderful Walnut Pie 162

■ Y ■

Yogurt, Frozen 147
York Brownies 48
You Won't Believe It
Isn't Potato Salad 98
Yuletide Eggnog Cake 122
Yum-Yum Casserole 75

■ Z ■

Zucchini Bars 42
Zucchini Beef Casserole 67
Zucchini Bread 11
Zucchini Marmalade 182
Zucchini Pie 163